Endorsements

One of our solemn responsibilities in our **day by day devotions** is to pray "for kings and all who are in authority" (I Timothy 2:2). In her book, *Praying for the President*, Dr. Pauline Hord, at 95 years of age and experience, challenges us to fulfill this divine mandate. God alone knows what would take place in our beloved land if Christians were to take this call to prayer seriously and persistently. We need a heaven sent revival before it is too late!

Dr Stephen F. Olford
FOUNDER AND CHAIRMAN – Olford Ministries International
SENIOR LECTURER – Stephen Olford Center for Biblical Preaching
Memphis, TN

Prayer is our greatest privilege as children of God. We need to pray daily and pray with focused prayers. I wholeheartedly commend this beautiful journal.

Dr Adrian Rogers
SENIOR PASTOR – Bellevue Baptist Church
Memphis, TN

Dr Pauline Hord is the most faithful prayer warrior I have ever known. Having her pray with me each Sunday morning before worship services is one of the greatest blessings of my life. May Pauline's book help America discover the truth of 2 Chronicles 7:14.

Dr Bill Bouknight
SENIOR PASTOR – Christ United Methodist Church
Memphis, TN

Here are my directions:
Pray much for others; plead for God's mercy upon them;
give thanks for all He is going to do for them.
Pray in this way for kings and for all others who
are in authority over us, or are in places of high
responsibility, so that we can live in peace and quietness,
spending our time in godly living and
thinking much about the Lord.

1 Timothy 2:1-2

Praying for the President

A Daily Guide of Scripture and Prayer

by Dr. Pauline Jones Hord

Praying for the President – A Daily Guide of Scripture and Prayer
ISBN 1-930285-13-2
First Edition First Printing (1000 copies)

Copyright©2002 by Dr. Pauline Jones Hord
Credits: Capitol Building on cover
　　© Getty Images, Seattle, WA, AA010332 (RF)
Published by The Master Design
　　PO Box 17865
　　Memphis, TN 38187-0865
　　Info@masterdesign.org

Additional copies may be purchased from the Master Design website
(www.masterdesign.org) or from:
　　The Pauline Hord Trust
　　2095 Exeter Rd #80-200
　　Germantown, TN 38138

Unless otherwise noted, Scripture quotations are from The Living Bible,
copyright © 1971 by Tyndale House Publishers, Wheaton, Illinois. All
rights reserved.

Printed by Bethany Press International in the USA.

JJ

Dedication

This book is dedicated to my special mentor of many years, Dr. Frank Laubach. He was one of ten acclaimed saints of the last century. Dr. Laubach was not only the world's greatest literacy teacher but a mighty man of prayer.

Acknowledgments

I wish to first give thanks to Janet Sheahan, the person who above all others brought this publication into existence.

I am also greatly indebted to the seven special prayer partners who put my handwritten manuscript onto a computer for publishing. They are Rebecca Carter, Pat Coe, Betty Cook, Joy Everett, Katie Howse, Kim Henley and Paula Morehard. Also I wish to express my gratitude for the encouragement and personal help given me by Mary Lou Liming.

Foreword

I never will forget the only occasion when I was present in an audience with the President of the United States. President George W. Bush had just returned from one of his early visits with President Putin of Russia. It was an unscripted meeting and the President talked "off the cuff." I was tremendously impressed by the genuine, even passionate, expression of his Christian faith.

He told us that 90% of the people who speak to him, or have the opportunity to greet him, always say to him, "Mr. President, I'm praying for you." He added that this was one of the most meaningful aspects of his life as President and confessed how desperately he needed our prayers.

Then he added a very interesting observation: "As you know, I've just returned from a visit with President Putin and some leaders of other countries. As I met with him, I could not help but wonder if he had people praying for him as I have praying for me."

President Bush then shared about how he lives with Scripture every day and spends time in morning prayer – how he is dependent upon the prayers of people.

It is especially meaningful for me to introduce and endorse Pauline Hord's book, *Praying for the President*. Pauline is one of the three or four most outstanding "prayer warriors" I know. Throughout my ministry in Memphis, where I was her pastor for twelve years, she was a bulwark of strength for my wife and me and our family. Even now, years later, when there is a special need in our lives, Jerry and I call Pauline.

I know that these prayers come from a heart of *passion* for prayer and a heart of *compassion* for the leadership of our nation. If millions of people could use this little book of prayers to focus their praying for the President, I am convinced that it would bring a spiritual revolution. When we pray in an intercessory kind of way, we not only participate in unleashing God's power for the persons for whom we pray, but something happens to us. We are bound together in God's spiritual enterprise of saving the world.

Prayer is God's idea. In His sovereignty, He engages us, in fact is dependent upon us, to share in His Kingdom enterprise through prayer. I often ask the question, "What if there are some things God either cannot or will not do until and unless people pray?" That does not in any way question God's sovereignty or power. It simply underscores the role God has designed for each of us in His Kingdom enterprise. God calls us to pray. Pauline has responded to His call and gives us a very helpful resource to pray in a focused and effective way for our President.

Maxie Dunnam
President, Asbury Theological Seminary

Introduction

Praying for the President is a publication which has evolved since 1977 when God spoke to my heart that I should support my new President in daily prayer. *Prayers for the President* was a book written beginning with the first day of Jimmy Carter's inauguration, January 21, 1977. In the year 2002 that book was rewritten and published under the title, *Praying for the President*. I hope this book will be used as a handbook to encourage our people to pray daily for our President. Our Lord has urged us to do this in I Timothy 2:2. One of the deep desires of my heart is that the Christian and God-loving people of America will unite in daily prayer for our President, the administration and our nation.

Pauline Jones Hord
Memphis, TN

A Prayer for Our Beloved Country

Dear Father,

As I now keep, with many others, a prayer vigil
For our beloved country, I praise Your holy name.
Your blessed Self,
You, who are the Creator of the Universe,
Maker of all that is,
Lord and Ruler of all that has life,
I kneel before You in adoration,
in praise, in thanksgiving,
to glorify You,
to magnify You,
in my heart, and in my mind.
Not just in this hour,
not just for a day,
nor for a week, nor a month,
but forever and ever and ever
throughout eternity.
Along with other American Christians
I acknowledge before your throne of grace
the sins and transgressions
of myself, and all others
who have lived and do live
in this glorious and blessed land.
You, our Lord, our God,
have given us a magnificent and beautiful country
and have blessed us with abundance
in all the resources of Your creation.

But we have been a negligent, and unappreciative people,
   reaping where we sowed not,
      often laying waste by profligate use
         bounties from Your abundance
            which we did not need nor deserve.
We have been guilty of many sins –
   of taking more than we needed,
      of wasting more than we used,
         of ruining more than we replaced.
And we acknowledge these and other sins
   and during these hours, day and night,
      we plead for your forgiveness –
And now on bended knee,
   in the stillness of the night,
      we search our hearts
         for signs of true repentance.
Help us, O Lord,
   to see ourselves as You see us,
      to know ourselves as You know us –
And then to be made aware completely
   of the multitudinous ways
      in which we have failed You
         during the two hundred years
            in which we have been a free people,
               a nation pledged to be Your people,
                  blessed beyond all lands
                     by Your munificent hands,
                        which have poured out upon us
                           such wealth, and such abundance,
                              and such blessings,
                                 as few nations, or perhaps no nation,
                                    has ever enjoyed.

You have blessed us
   with liberty and leadership
      with food and fuel in abundance,
         with beauty in every form.
You have protected us,
   blessed us, saved us, guided us,
      and preserved us throughout two centuries –
Please, O Lord,
   continue to be our Lord,
      our Protector, our Shield –
Save our nation and our people
   from the sins of ingratitude,
      of wastefulness,
         of selfishness,
            of indifference.
And restore to us the attributes
   of mind and heart
      which once made us great in leadership
         and united us in purposeful achievement.
Amen.

January 1

Jeremiah 1:4-5

The Lord said to me, "I knew you before you were formed within your mother's womb: before you were born I sanctified you and appointed you as my spokesman to the world."

Prayer

Dear Lord God, Father of all mankind, permit me to enter into Your Holy Presence, that at Your throne of grace I may once again submit the name of my President as an object of Your divine love. You are so dear to my soul this first day of a new year. You flood my heart and mind with a sweet and precious insight that in these very words of Jeremiah You reestablish that our President is well-known to You. You created him, chose him, planned for him to be a spokesman for You. Thank You, Father.

My Concerns Today

_____
_____
_____
_____

January 2

Proverbs 16:7

When a man is trying to please God, God makes even his worst enemies to be at peace with him.

Prayer

Dear Lord God, Father of all nations and Judge of all people, We humbly pray this day for our President. His desire is to please You. He longs for peace on earth as millions of Your children do. We pray for peace. But teach us, O Lord, that the world can have peace only when we have a willingness to know their tragic needs and a determination to help them meet their needs. Christ came to bring abundant life, not just to America or the white man, but to all men of all nations. O God, bless our President, as he, the symbol of America, appears before other nations. In Christ's name I pray.

My Concerns Today

_____
_____
_____
_____

January 3

Ephesians 6:10

I want to remind you that your strength must come from the Lord's mighty power within you.

Prayer

Dear God, our Father and Source of all life, we humbly bow in mind and heart to the knowledge that any strength we have to do good, comes from Your power. As our President confers with other leaders this day, may he be affirming constantly with his total inner self: "the strength I need is within me – the might power of the Lord; physical endurance is mine; divine guidance is available; reassurance of purpose is being given me, now; all by the mighty power of my Lord's indwelling." In Christ's name I pray.

January 4

Isaiah 61:11

The Lord will show the nations of the world His justice; His righteousness shall be like a budding tree...springing up everywhere.

Prayer

Dear Lord, God of all nations, You are fair to all people, giving equal opportunity to all to see Your righteousness. In this early morning hour I praise You for revealing to these leaders – our President and others – Your holiness and righteousness. As they talk together today, may Your Spirit be in control. Affirm in each, Your Presence, as they seek commitment to achieving justice for all the people. As they stand firm in their faith, may they strengthen one another. In Christ's holy name I pray.

My Concerns Today

_____

_____

_____

_____

My Concerns Today

_____

_____

_____

_____

January 5

James 5:13,18

If you are wise, live a life of steady goodness, so that only good deeds will pour forth...And those who are peacemakers will plant seeds of peace and reap a harvest of goodness.

Prayer

Dear Lord, whose Son came to bring peace and love, teach us and our national leaders ways of peace. All praise is due to Your holiness that our President is a man of peace and is willing to be used in Your plans for peace among nations. Let those who are informed only by the media be patient with our leaders and sensitive to their need of support through prayer. May the nation be aware of Your concern for all people and be ever mindful of the needs of others. In Christ's name I pray.

January 6

Philippians 1:11

May you always be doing those good kind things which show that you are a child of God, for this will bring much praise and glory to the Lord.

Prayer

Dear Lord, praise be to Your Holiness that You have endowed man with such potential nobility of soul – that he can be sensitive to the suffering of others and grateful for their gracious gifts – mindful of his own mission on earth – and obedient to divine orders. Only the Almighty could have endowed man with such capabilities. As our President visits other countries during his presidency, be with him. May he reflect the Spirit of Your Son, in whose name I pray.

My Concerns Today

_____
_____
_____
_____

My Concerns Today

_____
_____
_____
_____

January 7

Colossians 2:6-7

And now just as you trusted Christ to save you, trust Him, too, for each day's problems; live in vital union with Him. Let your roots grow down into Him and draw up nourishment from Him.

Prayer

Dear Lord God, who commands the angels and blesses us through them, our people are grateful this day for the care of our President. He needs rest but is faced with great responsibilities. He needs quietness, but he is faced with extreme unrest among some groups in our country. As he comes to You, the Source of all strength, give him this day the energy, vitality and strength of mind and body he so sorely needs. O Lord, give him abundant nourishment, in Your Son's name and for His glory.

My Concerns Today

_____
_____
_____
_____

January 8

1 Peter 5:7

Let Him have all your worries and cares, for He is always thinking about you and watching everything that concerns you.

Prayer

Dear Lord, who watches over all creation, we praise and worship You. In the midst of this confusing, baffling economic situation I ask that You will give to the proper leaders sound advice for our President. It is all so complex I cannot understand. But I know You have all the solutions, O Lord. May our President cast all worries upon You – relying fully for wisdom and guidance to come from You. Bless our people, O Lord, who look to You for strength, courage, and wisdom. In Christ's name I pray.

My Concerns Today

_____
_____
_____
_____

John 6:29

Jesus told them, "This is the will of God, that you believe in the One He has sent."

Prayer

Dear Lord God, how wonderfully Your Son fulfills our every need. We praise You for sending Him to us. This day I pray that our President may look to our Lord for the fulfilling of every need. Let him hear the Savior say, "I am the Bread of Life….Those believing in Me will never thirst….I am you Comforter. I have sent My Spirit to be with you always….I am your Teacher. Learn of Me….I am the Way. Follow Me….I am your Shepherd. You shall not want." Thank You, Heavenly Father, for Your Son. In His name I pray.

Luke 4:8

Jesus replied, "We must worship God and Him alone. So it is written in the Scriptures."

Prayer

Dear Lord God, we praise You for the revelation of Yourself through the words of Your Son. O Lord, send a mighty revival of the study of Your Holy Word to the people of our nation. Make our minds and hearts receive the teachings of the Master. Our President and his administration can only lead the people to do what is righteous when the people acknowledge what is righteous – what Your will is – not our selfish wills, individually and/or collectively. Heal our nation, O Lord! Turn our faces toward You, O God! In Christ's name I pray.

My Concerns Today

_____
_____
_____
_____

My Concerns Today

_____
_____
_____
_____

Job 32:8-9

But it is not mere age that makes men wise. Rather it is the spirit in a man, the breath of the Almighty which makes him intelligent.

Prayer

Dear Lord, our Father and our God, we know You are the Source of all intelligence. We thank You that the inspiration of the Almighty is available to any of us at any time. All matters can be handled through this inspiration. In using divine inspiration we develop the quality of our faith and know the joy of living life to the fullest. I pray this day that our President, each member of his Cabinet, and all members of the Administration will avail themselves of the use of this gift. May Your Spirit dwell in each of them assuring the use of divine inspiration. In His name I pray.

My Concerns Today

_____
_____
_____
_____

Matthew 7:12

Do for others what you want them to do for you.

Prayer

Dear Heavenly Father, Your Spirit speaks to my heart about the farmers of America. Please help our President, the Secretary of Agriculture, and others in official positions to solve this problem. The farmers feed us, and help to feed many other millions. And every farmer deserves a decent income. But many are losing money, not making money. I don't understand all the complexities. But I don't have to understand. Please, Lord, hear the prayers of Your people concerning this very serious problem. Give our leaders a solution. In Christ's name I pray.

My Concerns Today

_____
_____
_____
_____

Psalm 139:23-24

Search me, O God, and know my heart; test my thoughts. Point out anything You find in me that makes You sad, and lead me along the path of everlasting life.

Prayer

Dear Lord God, we thank You for establishing a means of communication between Yourself and man. We thank You that the Bible gives us examples of men who engaged in cognitive prayer. They saw truth for their personal lives and their national life because they saw Your truths known to You alone. Only when such leaders sought You in prayer could they receive revelation of Truth. In the name of Christ, I ask You to hear the prayers of our President, and his coworkers.

My Concerns Today

_____

_____

_____

_____

Joshua 4:24

He did this so that all the nations of the earth will realize that Jehovah is the mighty God, and so that all of you will worship Him.

Prayer

Dear Lord, God of all nations, I bow before You as the mighty God of many miracles. As You held back the waters of the Jordan River and the Red Sea, You can and do perform miracles today. I believe You have such a leader in our President (as You had in Joshua) and therefore I ask for some miracles during his administration. He made promises. You know them. Our people know them. He can only keep them through Your strength and power. In the name of our miracle-working Christ I pray for our President.

My Concerns Today

_____

_____

_____

_____

January 15

Psalm 34:1-3

I will praise the Lord no matter what happens...Let all who are discouraged take heart. Let us praise the Lord together, and exalt His name.

Prayer

Dear Lord, as I pray for our President today, I realize that there are days in which he may have sorrows and disappointments which are personal. Only his family and dearest friends may know his sadness and only they can truly mourn with him. May they turn their mourning into praise and joy. In Christ's name.

January 16

John 12:46

I have come as a Light to shine in this dark world, so that all who put their trust in Me will no longer wander in the darkness.

Prayer

Dear Lord, how brilliant is Your Light! How we, Your present-day disciples, thank You for it. Because of our sin we face such darkness. But Your Light never ceases. In lives such as martyrs of old it shines brightly – lighting the way for many others. Keep that eternal Light of Your spirit shining steadily and brightly in our President, we pray. As we trust in You, O Lord, may the light of faith, hope, and love shine brighter in each of us for we ask it in Christ's name and for His sake.

My Concerns Today

_____
_____
_____
_____

My Concerns Today

_____
_____
_____
_____

Proverbs 21:21

The man who tries to be good, loving, and kind finds life, righteousness, and honor.

Prayer

Dear Father, There are so many leaders and just average citizens we see and know are righteous. Keep us ever aware that You as our God expect that kind of life from all of us. I pray this day for our President. May he study and practice the truths You have taught us. In so doing he will find life, righteousness and honor as you promised. In Christ's name.

My Concerns Today

_____

_____

_____

_____

Psalm 37:37

For the good man – the blameless, the upright, the man of peace – he has a wonderful future ahead of him.

Prayer

Dear Father, You are so loving, so good to us. You nourish us through Your Word. Thank You for all the wonderful promises You have given us. The prayer of my heart today is that our President will remember such promises as this one in Psalm 37:37. Criticisms have been made. Some people have withheld their cooperation. But let him take heart as he recalls the words of Martin Luther: "And though this world, with devils filled, Should threaten to undo us, We will not fear for God hath willed His truth to triumph through us." In Christ's name I pray.

My Concerns Today

_____

_____

_____

_____

Isaiah 41:17

I will answer when they cry to Me. I, Israel's God, will not ever forsake them.

Prayer

Dear Lord God, what amazing promises You have made to Your people. We are Your people through our salvation by Christ. Hear the cries of Your people now. Throughout the world Your people are crying for peace. But You are Righteousness – Goodness – Justice. You cannot look upon sin. And all of us have sinned. Forgive us, Lord. Forgive our people. Forgive our leaders. Forgive our President. Cleanse him and make him Your true and perfect vessel for this day of need. In Christ's name.

Psalm 85:1,10

Lord, You have poured out amazing blessings on this land! Mercy and truth have met together. Grim justice and peace have kissed.

Prayer

Dear Lord, as through the ages men have praised You, so do I. You have poured out blessings upon us. As I pray for the President, the deep desire of my heart is that Your creative power will continue to move through him. May no self-will, no blind stupidity, no rebellious spirit in any individual or any group of Americans block Your creative leadership in the President. Make us, as individuals and our nation as a whole, what You want us to be. In Christ's holy name I pray.

My Concerns Today

_____
_____
_____
_____

My Concerns Today

_____
_____
_____
_____

January 21

Psalm 25:9,12

He will teach the ways that are right and best to those who humbly turn to Him. Where is the man who fears the Lord? God will teach him how to choose the best.

Prayer

Dear Lord, I pray this day that You will teach our President the ways that are right and best because he has turned to You in humility. On this day please let him and his dear wife sense Your presence. In Christ's name I pray.

January 22

Isaiah 62:4

For the Lord delights in you and will claim you as His own.

Prayer

Dear Lord, thank You, that You have claimed our President as Your own and that now You delight to work through him as a leader of Your people in America. In Christ's name.

My Concerns Today

_____

_____

_____

_____

My Concerns Today

_____

_____

_____

_____

Psalm 26:1,3

I have tried to keep Your laws and have trusted You without wavering…For I have taken Your loving kindness and Your truths as my ideals.

Prayer

Dear Lord, thank You that the President has tried to keep Your laws and has trusted You. Now I pray that he will constantly call upon You to check on his motives so that in all his duties and responsibilities he may ever keep loving kindness and truth as his ideals. In Christ's name.

My Concerns Today

_____
_____
_____
_____

Psalm 61:6,8

You will give me added years of life as rich and full as those of many generations, all packed into one…And I will praise Your name continually, fulfilling my vow of praising You each day.

Prayer

Dear Lord, give to the President added years of life, rich and full of successful service in which he will praise Your name because he believes in Your Truth and is guided by You as he daily draws strength and wisdom from Your unlimited storehouse. In Christ's name.

My Concerns Today

_____
_____
_____
_____

January 25

Psalm 66:20

Blessed be God who didn't turn away when I was praying, and didn't refuse me His kindness and love.

Prayer

Dear Lord, hallowed and praised be Your name that You have never turned away from Your servant, our President. Show him Your kindness and love when he prays under the direction of the Holy Spirit to You, our Father. In Christ's name I pray.

January 26

Psalm 28:7

He is my strength, my shield from every danger. I trusted in Him and He helped me.

Prayer

Dear Lord, our country has many needs at this time, but none more than a stalwart, praying Christian at the helm. Now we have this President chosen by the people. So I pray that daily You will be his joy, strength, and shield, and that he will continually praise You with his whole life. In Christ's name I pray.

My Concerns Today

_____
_____
_____
_____

My Concerns Today

_____
_____
_____
_____

Psalm 71:5,7

Oh, Lord, You alone are my hope; I've trusted You from childhood. My success—at which so many stand amazed—is because You are my mighty protector.

Prayer

Dear Lord, as we look upon the election of this president, we sense a work of divine plan. You chose him, trained him, nurtured and protected him for Your own divine purpose. May Your will be done in this nation and in the world through this man who is Your servant. In Christ's name.

Psalm 75:6-7

For promotion and power come from nowhere on earth, but only from God. He promotes one and deposes another.

Prayer

Dear Lord, You have promoted the President, Your servant, to a place of great power and You have done this miracle. Now I plead with You to keep him so humble before You that Your will may be accomplished through his life. In Christ's name I pray.

My Concerns Today

_____
_____
_____
_____

My Concerns Today

_____
_____
_____
_____

Hebrews 12:1

Since we have such a huge crowd of men of faith watching us from the grandstands, let us strip off anything that slows us down, or holds us back, and especially those sins that wrap themselves so tightly around our feet and trip us up, and let us run with patience the particular race that God has set before us.

Prayer

Dear Father, as the President now stands before the world as the leader of a Christian people, let all sins and weaknesses which bind him and us be washed away by Your Spirit that we as a nation may run the race according to Your purpose.

Hebrews 13:9

Your spirited strength comes as a gift from God.

Prayer

Dear Lord, we thank You for the spiritual strength with which You have endowed our President. May he daily do Your will and may his spiritual strength be so discernible that many others will step out boldly for You. In Christ's name.

My Concerns Today

_____

_____

_____

_____

My Concerns Today

_____

_____

_____

_____

Psalm 62:2

He alone is my rock, my rescuer, defense and fortress. Why then should I be tense with fear when troubles come?

Prayer

Dear Lord, in the time of any crisis, please keep our President's mind under Your control, that he may receive wisdom from on high in making vital and stupendous decisions. In Christ's name.

My Concerns Today

_____

_____

_____

_____

Psalm 68:35

The God of Israel gives strength and mighty power to His people. Blessed be God.

Prayer

Dear Lord, give daily strength and power to Your servant, our President, in the blessed name of Jesus.

Psalm 86:2-3

Protect me from death, for I try to follow all Your laws. Save me, for I am serving You and trusting You. Be merciful, O Lord, I am looking up to You in constant hope.

Prayer

Dear Lord, I pray that You will protect the President from all evil. Be merciful to him, O Lord. Give him strength and wisdom as he deals with the mighty issues of our national government and our relationships with all other nations. In Christ's name.

My Concerns Today

_____
_____
_____
_____

My Concerns Today

_____
_____
_____
_____

Jeremiah 29:11-13

"For I know the plans I have for you," says the Lord. "They are plans for good and not for evil, to give you a future and a hope. In those days when you pray, I will listen. You will find Me when you seek Me, if you look for Me in earnest."

Prayer

Dear Lord, we know You have great plans for our country under the leadership of the President if his mind and will are constantly in the attitude of prayer. So I pray that he will continuously seek Your Will with all his heart. In Christ's name.

John 9:4-5

All of us must quickly carry out the tasks assigned us by the One who sent Me, for there is little time left before the night falls and all work comes to an end. But while I am still here in the world I give it My light.

Prayer

Dear Lord, I pray that as You gave light through the Spirit of the Lord Jesus to His apostles, You will now give Your light to the mind and heart of the President, that he may carry out successfully the tasks You have assigned to him for the next four years, for the good of our nation and the world and for Christ's sake.

My Concerns Today

_____

_____

_____

_____

My Concerns Today

_____

_____

_____

_____

February 5

Psalm 89:24

I will protect and bless him constantly and surround him with My love; he will be great because of Me.

Prayer

Dear Lord, may the people of our land pray daily for Your protection of our President. I plead with You that he will be blessed and protected by Your love every hour. In the name of Christ, our Savior I pray.

February 6

Matthew 6:34

So don't be anxious about tomorrow. God will take care of you tomorrow, too. Live one day at a time.

Prayer

Dear Lord, let the President never be anxious about the tomorrows – the future weeks and months – but keep his mind so clearly under Your control that he can deal with today, each day, one day at a time. We know You have the future in Your hands and under Your control. In Christ's name.

My Concerns Today

_____

_____

_____

_____

My Concerns Today

_____

_____

_____

_____

1 Timothy 1:5

What I am eager for is that all the Christians will be filled with love that comes from pure hearts, and that their minds will be clear and their faith strong.

Prayer

Dear Lord, I pray all the Christians in our governmental bodies in Washington will be filled with love and led by Your Spirit, to the end that under the leadership of the President, they may unite to do Your holy will in their political as well as their private lives. In Christ's name.

2 Timothy 2:1-2

Be strong with the strength Christ Jesus gives you. For you must teach others those things you and many others have heard me speak about. Teach these great truths to trustworthy men who will in turn pass them on to others.

Prayer

Dear Lord, since You chose the President through the voice of the people to be our President, I pray in Christ's name that You will keep him faithful in his search for Your Truth. May he pass on such truth and understanding from You to others for the building of Your Kingdom on earth.

My Concerns Today

_____
_____
_____
_____

My Concerns Today

_____
_____
_____
_____

February 9

Isaiah 59:1

The Lord isn't too weak to save you. And He isn't deaf. He can hear you when you call.

Prayer

Dear Lord, we know You hear our people calling to You to redeem us. Renew us as a nation with Your Spirit and give Your most divine blessings of wisdom and courage in leadership to our President. In Christ's name.

February 10

Isaiah 58:13-14

If you keep the Sabbath day holy...honoring the Lord in what you do...not following your own desires and pleasure...I will see to it that you get your full share of blessings. The Lord has spoken.

Prayer

Dear Lord, we thank You that You have brought to the White House a Bible-reading Christian man - our President. May Your Holy Word constantly reestablish Your truths in his heart. In Christ's name.

My Concerns Today

_____

_____

_____

_____

My Concerns Today

_____

_____

_____

_____

February 11

Ecclesiastes 11:7

It is a wonderful thing to be alive.

Prayer

Dear Lord, we thank You that our President is so alive - so filled with health in body, mind, and spirit. Bless him with renewed strength daily that he may deal efficiently with the numerous responsibilities which rest upon him. In Christ's name.

February 12

Isaiah 44:21

Pay attention Israel, for you are My servant; I made you and I will not forget to help you.

Prayer

Dear Father, I know You made the President. I know he is Your servant. You are helping him with his words, attitudes, and relationships with the other leaders. We praise Your holy name that this is true. In Christ's name, we pray.

My Concerns Today

_____
_____
_____
_____

My Concerns Today

_____
_____
_____
_____

February 13

Isaiah 45:3

And I will give you treasures hidden in the darkness, secret riches; and you will know that I am doing this - I, the Lord, the God of Israel, the One who calls you by your name.

Prayer

O Lord God, the treasures we pray You will give to our President are treasures of understanding Your plan for him, for our country, and for the world as we move on toward the coming of Your kingdom on earth. In Christ's name we pray.

February 14

John 15:16

You didn't choose Me! I chose you! I appointed you to go and produce lovely fruit always - so that no matter what you ask for from the Father, using My name, He will give it to you.

Prayer

Dear Lord, we know that You have chosen the President, and appointed him to bear fruit in Your Kingdom. Therefore we pray daily that You will meet every need he has as he works for the national good. In Christ's name.

My Concerns Today

_____
_____
_____
_____

My Concerns Today

_____
_____
_____
_____

Psalm 96:10

Tell the nations that Jehovah reigns! He rules the world. His power can never be overthrown. He will judge all nations fairly.

Prayer

Dear Father, we thank You that our President knows Your Holy Word and that he believes You when You say You are all powerful. If our people and our leaders who know You as Father God will acknowledge You, I know You will protect AND BLESS US. In Christ's name I pray for our nation.

Psalm 97:2,6

Righteousness and justice are the foundations of His throne. The heavens declare His perfect righteousness; every nation sees His glory.

Prayer

Dear Father, in the name of Jesus Christ, let righteousness and justice so permeate the thinking and the spoken words of the President that all who deal with him in the Oval Office or in the Congress may feel the impact of Your Spirit in their deliberations. May other nations see Your glory prevailing in our land. In Christ's name.

My Concerns Today

_____
_____
_____
_____

My Concerns Today

_____
_____
_____
_____

John 15:1-2

I am the true vine and my Father is the Gardner. He lops off every branch that doesn't produce.

Prayer

Dear Father, we know You do not approve of waste, and we are guilty as individuals and as a nation. We ask forgiveness for this sin. Bless the President and his coworkers in their cutting and pruning of our complicated government structure. May all of it be to Your ultimate glory. In Christ's name.

John 14:23

Jesus replied, "I will only reveal Myself to those who love Me and obey Me."

Prayer

Dear Lord, keep the President faithful in his love and obedience to You that You may continue to reveal to him Your solutions for these complex problems of State. In Christ's name.

My Concerns Today

_____
_____
_____
_____

My Concerns Today

_____
_____
_____
_____

February 19

Psalm 27:11

Tell me what to do, O Lord, and make it plain because I am surrounded by waiting enemies.

Prayer

Dear Lord, all kinds of enemies surround Your servant, the President, plotting to ensnare him as quickly as possible. We, who speak Your name many times daily in prayer, plead for Your protective angels to keep him safely in the paths of righteousness. Surround him with a wall of protection from all physical and spiritual harm, which the evil one exerts against him. In Christ's name I pray.

My Concerns Today

_____
_____
_____
_____

February 20

Psalm 57:9

I will thank You publicly throughout the land. I will sing Your praises among the nations.

Prayer

Dear Lord, please guard the President's mind and spirit from even the slightest fear of ridicule or criticism as he lifts up Jesus Christ Your Son. You are God of all creation. You are mightier than all men. Whatever the spirits are that abide in the breasts of his enemies they will surely bow down when You are lifted up. In Christ's name.

My Concerns Today

_____
_____
_____
_____

Psalm 60:12

With God's help we shall do mighty things, for He will trample down our foes.

Prayer

Dear Lord, bless the President and all our national leaders with pure motives and deeds of integrity, that our nation may do mighty things for those who follow You through the world. Let the downhearted and discouraged of other lands take courage when they behold the things of goodness and honor done by American leaders. In Christ's name.

Psalm 27:7-8

Listen to my pleading, Lord: Be merciful and send the help I need. My heart has heard You say, "Come and talk with Me, O My people." And my heart responds, "Lord, I am coming."

Prayer

Dear Lord, hear the cries for help which rise from the heart and lips of the President. His heart ascends daily to You in supplication and trust. I know You will never fail him. Awaken, O God, in all of us who love and trust You, a deeper commitment to support our President with our love, respect, prayers, and cooperation. In Christ's name.

My Concerns Today

_____
_____
_____
_____

My Concerns Today

_____
_____
_____
_____

Joshua 1:9

Yes, be bold and strong. Banish fear and doubt! For remember, the Lord your God is with you wherever you go.

Prayer

Dear Lord, bless the President today with boldness and strength to do Your will whatever the consequences. Our nation needs Your guidance, O Lord, please give it. The nations of the world need to respect us for the truths we stand for and live by. Therefore, O Lord, we pray for special strength and boldness in our President in standing for all that is morally right. In Christ's name.

Psalm 65:5

O God who saves us, You are the only hope of all mankind throughout the world and far away upon the sea.

Prayer

Dear Lord, as the President proclaims this in his heart - that You are the only hope of mankind - please bless him with Your all-wise counsel as to his words and deeds in his dealing with the leaders of other nations. In Christ's name.

My Concerns Today

_____
_____
_____
_____

My Concerns Today

_____
_____
_____
_____

February 25

Psalm 31:21

Blessed is the Lord, for He has shown me that His never-failing love protects me like the walls of a fort.

Prayer

Dear Lord, I praise Your Holy Name for blessing the President with a sense of Your presence so that he stands before the Press with confidence, assurance and serenity as he answers their questions. Yet he always speaks with simplicity and humility. Thank You Father, for Your controlling Presence in him. In Christ's name.

February 26

Psalm 51:6

You deserve honesty from the heart; yes, utter sincerity and truthfulness. Oh, give me this wisdom.

Prayer

Dear Lord, how we thank You for a national leader who reads and teaches Your Holy Word. Bless the President with renewed wisdom and faithfulness in divining the marvelous truths from Your Holy Word. As he reads and studies Your Word may the truths You reveal become ever more meaningful to him as he deals with the affairs of government. In Christ's name.

My Concerns Today

_____
_____
_____
_____

My Concerns Today

_____
_____
_____
_____

Psalm 51:11-12

Don't take Your Holy Spirit from me - make me willing to obey You.

Prayer

Dear Lord, bless the President as he deals with every emergency. May Your words be spoken through our President's lips that Your Word may go out to protect the innocent in every nation and return to You with the fruit for the Kingdom. Give our President boldness and courage in the face of evil. And hallowed be Your name forever.

Deuteronomy 13:3-4

The Lord is testing you to find out whether or not you really love Him with all your heart and soul. You must never worship any God but Jehovah; obey only His commands and cling to Him.

Prayer

Dear Lord, so fill the President's entire being with a sense of Your Presence that he will truly be a man who "walks and talks with God." As he does this, may Your direction of this nation become a reality. In Christ's name.

My Concerns Today

_____

_____

_____

_____

My Concerns Today

_____

_____

_____

_____

March 1

Isaiah 66:2

I will look with pity on the man who has a humble and a contrite heart, who trembles at My word.

Prayer

Dear Lord, we pray for our President to be a man with a humble and a contrite heart. Inspire him to study and teach Your Holy Word. Therefore, we praise You that our nation is now being led by such a man and we ask Your blessing upon him. In Christ's name.

March 2

2 Samuel 22:27-28

To those who are pure, You show yourself pure; but You destroy those who are evil. You save those in trouble, but You bring down the haughty; for You watch their every move.

Prayer

Dear Lord, thank You for sending out Your strong and courageous voice through the President. We praise Your holy name again for the President who allows You to use him for Your purposes. With divine boldness he stands for the right through Your strength in him.

My Concerns Today

_____

_____

_____

_____

My Concerns Today

_____

_____

_____

_____

2 Samuel 22:31-33

As for God, His way is perfect; The word of the Lord is true. He shields all who hide behind Him. Our Lord alone is God: We have no other Savior. God is my strong fortress.

Prayer

Dear Lord, keep the President hiding always behind You and Your Holy Word – trusting only in Your Power and righteousness. Through Your laws of justice and morality strengthen our nation always to withstand the onslaught of various enemies. In Christ's name.

Psalm 42:11

O my soul, don't be discouraged. Don't be upset. Expect God to act! For I know that I shall again have plenty of reason to praise Him for all that He will do. He is my help. He is my God!

Prayer

Dear Lord, on the days when the President might feel discouragement and heartache because of the lack of progress in the affairs, cause him to look to You again in confidence. Fill his mind and heart with Your holy promises. You are his Source as You are mine. You are his Help. You are his God. May he claim Your promises daily.

My Concerns Today

_____
_____
_____
_____

My Concerns Today

_____
_____
_____
_____

Luke 10:27

You must love the Lord your God with all your heart, and with all your soul, and with all your strength, and with all your mind. And you must love your neighbor just as much as you love yourself.

Prayer

Dear Lord, help the President this day to have the patience and the wisdom to deal well with each person who reaches him by phone. We thank You, Father, that our President cares enough about the problems and the thinking of the common man to try to hear their questions and understand their thinking. In Christ's name we pray for his responses and for the citizens who call him.

My Concerns Today

———————————————
———————————————
———————————————
———————————————

Psalm 138:3

When I pray, You answer me, and encourage me by giving me the strength I need.

Prayer

Dear Lord, the amount of strength needed by the President is known only to You. No other president, even as sympathetic as each might be with this President, could know his needs on this day at this hour. Only You, blessed Lord, know his needs. We believe Your promises and therefore trust You to fulfill every need as You have promised. In Christ's name.

My Concerns Today

———————————————
———————————————
———————————————
———————————————

Psalm 67:7-8,10

O God when You led your people through the wilderness, the earth trembled and the heavens shook. You sent abundant rain upon Your land, O God, to refresh it in its weariness.

Prayer

Dear Lord, You have done miraculous things for Your people down through the ages. We have read of these miracles. During wars, Your miracles have saved Your people, protected them, fed them, met their urgent needs. Now the President is faced with varied problems of our nation. Give him wisdom, O Lord.

Isaiah 65:1-2

The Lord says: people who never before inquired about Me are now seeking Me out. Nations who never before searched for Me are finding Me.

Prayer

Dear Lord, may the experiences our leaders and our news people have as they observe the President be of such interest and revelation that they too will seek You out. As more and more of his actions and words reflect Your Spirit, may more of Your children throughout the world search for You and find You. You are the only true and almighty God.

My Concerns Today

_____

_____

_____

_____

My Concerns Today

_____

_____

_____

_____

Psalm 73:27-28

Those refusing to worship God will perish, for He destroys those serving other gods. But as for me, I get as close to Him as I can!

Prayer

Dear Lord God, bless the President as he draws closer to You every day. We trust he will do this because his demeanor is that of one who knows his Redeemer, trusts Him, and walks with Him daily as he seeks counsel and strength. Let no false god take the President's mind and eye off of You, the Holy God. You are our nation's salvation.

Psalm 75:10

"I will cut off the strength of evil men," says the Lord, " and increase the power of good men in their place."

Prayer

Dear Lord, bless the President with added strength and courage daily to withstand the evil forces which we see in evidence in the actions of the terrorists in our nation's capitol. And we pray with our President for the safety of the hostages - innocent people - now being held prisoners by the "evil men." Oh, Lord, cut off their strength. In Christ's name.

My Concerns Today

_____
_____
_____
_____

My Concerns Today

_____
_____
_____
_____

Isaiah 2:6

The Lord has rejected you because you welcome foreigners from the East who practice magic and communicate with evil spirits.

Prayer

Dear Lord, do not reject America because we have welcomed foreigners from the East. Many have come with false teachings. Show the President and our national leaders what can and should be done to protect our Christian young people from entering into evil practices. In Christ's name.

Isaiah 6:8

Then I heard the Lord asking, "Whom shall I send as a messenger to My people? Who will go?" And I said, "Lord, I'll go. Send me."

Prayer

Dear Lord, thank You again that the President heard Your call to political life and was willing to trust You and say, "Lord, send me." As a citizen of this great country I prayed for a strong Christian leader. I'm sure many prayed for the same thing to happen. You heard our prayers. You called this servant of Yours. He was willing to say "Yes, Dear Lord, send me no matter the cost." Thank You, Father.

My Concerns Today

_____
_____
_____
_____

My Concerns Today

_____
_____
_____
_____

March 13

Isaiah 8:13

Don't fear anything except the Lord of the armies of heaven! If you fear Him, you need fear nothing else.

Prayer

Dear Lord, we know You are the Lord of all the armies of heaven. We know also that not only are You the Creator of the universe, but You have control over all the universe as well as heaven itself. We pray that our President will always have in his heart the fear of You, His Lord, which truly is the beginning of wisdom. For Your holy grace to be shed upon him daily, I pray in the name of Christ.

March 14

Hebrews 4:12

For whatever God says to us is full of loving power.

Prayer

Dear Father God, there are so many problems being presented daily to the mind of the President. I beseech You to send ample wisdom and abundant power to him through Your Holy Word. Grant to him the power to discern Your Truth when and as it comes to him through other avenues - whether that be through friends, enemies or circumstances. In Christ's name.

My Concerns Today

_____

_____

_____

_____

My Concerns Today

_____

_____

_____

_____

Colossians 3:15

Let the peace of heart which comes from Christ be always present in your hearts and lives, for this is your responsibility and privilege as members of His body.

Prayer

Dear Lord, we know as Christians that when we affirm that we are centered and poised in Christ we feel strengthened and assured. We feel fearless and confident. We feel peaceful and serene. As I pray for the President, I give You thanks that nothing can disturb the calm peace of his soul, because he is centered in Christ Himself. Bless him for Christ's sake.

My Concerns Today

_____

_____

_____

John 11:41-42

Father, thank You for hearing Me. You always hear Me.

Prayer

Dear Father God, we know You always heard the prayers of Your sinless Son. But also, Father, because of our precious Savior, we know You have promised to hear our prayers too. And so at this time, we think of the President with love. In faith, we surround him with our prayers. We trust him to You, our God, to bless him and protect him in every experience and under all circumstances. Your love for him will never fail and so we thank You. In Christ's name.

My Concerns Today

_____

_____

_____

March 17

Psalm 71:14

I will keep on expecting You to help me. I praise You more and more. I cannot count the times when You have faithfully rescued me from danger. I will tell everyone how good You are, and of Your constant daily care. I walk in the strength of the Lord God.

Prayer

Dear Lord, we thank You for the times when without anyone knowing it You have sent Your protecting angels to safeguard the President. We daily trust him to Your omnipotent and loving care. We beseech You also to surround each member of his family with loving and protective care. In Christ's name.

March 18

Psalm 40:8

And I delight to do Your will, my God, for Your law is written upon my heart.

Prayer

Dear Lord, the President has proclaimed that Your law is written upon his heart and he delights to do Your will. Therefore, I pray that in all circumstances, where he needs to know Your will in order to make a decision, You will be there meeting his need. Bless his family and may each proclaim You in his or her life. In Christ's name.

My Concerns Today

_____

_____

_____

_____

My Concerns Today

_____

_____

_____

_____

Psalm 40:16

But may the joy of the Lord be given to everyone who loves Him and His salvation. May they constantly exclaim, "How great God is"!

Prayer

Dear Father, the President knows how great You are. By his very life, may he proclaim to all people throughout the world that You are the one and only almighty God. May his stands on human rights proclaim every person is Your creation, and therefore each person is precious. Bless and protect him, O God, in Christ's name as he speaks out on human rights. In Christ's name I pray.

1 Chronicles 29:12

Riches and honor come from You alone, and You are the Ruler of all mankind; Your hand controls power and might, and it is at Your discretion that men are made great and given strength.

Prayer

Dear Lord, we know You are the Ruler of all mankind and we realize that You have control over all things of the earth as well as of the universe. That is why I pray constantly that You will keep the President intent on obeying every counsel and guidance You give him. Since You alone can make him truly great, give him the unlimited strength of mind, body, and spirit which he needs. In Christ's name.

My Concerns Today

_____
_____
_____
_____

My Concerns Today

_____
_____
_____
_____

March 21

Psalm 32:10

Abiding love surrounds those who trust in the Lord.

Prayer

Dear Father, may Your Holy Spirit completely surround and control the President and his wife, children and all his family. Bless him as he continues to stand up boldly for human rights. Protect him and all his family from harm which might be perpetrated by enemies of righteousness. Evil forces are so formidable, O God, that only in Your power which is greater, can we place our trust for his safety. In Christ's name I pray.

March 22

Psalm 145:15,19

The eyes of all mankind look up to You for help; He fulfills the desires of those who reverence and trust Him; He hears their cries for help and rescues them.

Prayer

Dear Lord, may Your Holy Spirit turn the eyes of all mankind toward You, our Almighty God. We seek Your divine help in these troubled times. O Lord, bless the President as he seeks to reverence Your holy name and trust You for divine guidance. Hear the cries of all Your people, O Lord, and send help to meet their various needs, physical and spiritual. In Christ's name.

My Concerns Today

_____

_____

_____

_____

My Concerns Today

_____

_____

_____

_____

Psalm 50:14-15

What I want from you is your true thanks; I want your promises fulfilled. I want you to trust Me in your times of trouble, so I can rescue you, and you can give Me glory.

Prayer

Dear Lord, bless the President as he seeks diligently to keep his campaign promises. No doubt he made them after much study, prayer, and guidance through Your Holy Spirit. Now, I pray You will enable him to keep those promises through further guidance from You and that You will give him strength of will for righteousness. O God, we pray for the leaders of other nations to also seek You and your righteousness.

1 Samuel 10:9

God gave him a new attitude.

Prayer

Dear Lord, You know better than anyone what happened when our President's attitude became pleasing to You. We thank you for our President's "new attitude." We praise You that he is Yours and he is not ashamed to say so. His commitment and dependency upon You is a blessing for our land.

My Concerns Today

_____

_____

_____

_____

My Concerns Today

_____

_____

_____

_____

March 25

Mark 10:43

Whoever wants to be great among you, must be your servant.

Prayer

Dear Lord, we believe the President wants to be Your servant. So on bended knee I pray daily for this man who is Your servant, that he may serve this nation and the world as You direct him. In Christ's name.

March 26

Joshua 24:15

As for me and my family, we will serve the Lord.

Prayer

Dear Lord, we pray the President's decision is to serve You – and no other god. Thank You for his parents who set the example and gave the training to their son in the years past – that son who is now our President – a leader that many nations of the world will look to for moral leadership. You have prepared him for, and brought him to, this hour. We pray that his family choses to serve You. In Christ's name.

My Concerns Today

_____

_____

_____

_____

My Concerns Today

_____

_____

_____

_____

Ecclesiastes 5:9

Oh, for a king who is devoted to his country; Only he can bring order from this chaos.

Prayer

Dear Lord, bless our President who is trying to bring order out of a very chaotic system of governemnt. Bless him with ideas about what should be done. Bless him with wisdom to share these ideas with others. Bless those who must help him to achieve the results. Bless all those with additional strength needed each day to achieve the ends they envision. In Christ's name.

Ecclesiastes 7:18

Tackle every task that comes along, and if you fear God you can expect His blessing.

Prayer

Dear Lord, our President is attcking each task in order of importance as he sees each need of our people. We pray that You will give him discernment to recognize the problems, wisdom to understand the problems, courage in the initiation of the solution, patience with his coworkers, and above all complete trust in Your gracious and constant help. In Christ's name I pray.

My Concerns Today

_____

_____

_____

_____

My Concerns Today

_____

_____

_____

_____

Ecclesiastes 12:13

Fear God and obey His commandments, for this is the entire dury of man.

Prayer

Dear Lord, as I consider this duty of man to obey Your commandments, I lift up our President to Your throne of grace. May Your commandments come first in his heart. I pray that the complexities of many involvements in government activities will not distort His commitments. May he follow You. In Christ's name I pray.

Psalm 66:7

Because of His great power He rules forever. He watches every movement of the nations. O rebel lands, He will deflate your pride.

Prayer

Dear Lord, I pray that You, Almighty and Holy God, will deflate the pride of the rebel lands around the world. Bless our President with knowledge and patience in dealing with leaders from these countries. We pray that he will not lose heart in his battle for human rights and peace. We pray that he will wear the banner of our Lord. In Christ's name.

My Concerns Today

_____

_____

_____

_____

My Concerns Today

_____

_____

_____

_____

Psalm 31:1,2,5

Lord, I trust in You alone. Answer quickly when I cry to You. Be for me a great rock of safety from my foes. Into Your hand I commit my spirit.

Prayer

Dear Lord God, for the sake of Christ and the advancement of Your kingdom I pray that our President will trust in You – will commit his spirit into Your hands daily. I pray that You will answer his cries for help in doing Your work in this world. Be his Protector and Comforter always.

My Concerns Today

_____

_____

_____

_____

1 Kings 10:9

Blessed be the Lord your God, Who chose you and set you on the throne of Israel. How the Lord must love Israel – for He gave you to them as their king! And You give Your people a just, good government.

Prayer

Dear Lord, I pray that as You have chosen the President for our leader that You will bless him with wisdom as You blessed King Solomon. He will thereby be able to help our nation become a just and good government, putting the practice of righteousness above the amassing of wealth.

Psalm 24:3-5

Who may stand before the Lord? Only those with pure hands and hearts, who do not practice dishonesty or lying. They will receive God's own goodness as their blessing from Him, planted in their lives by God Himself, their Savior.

Prayer

Dear Lord God, we ask You this day to plant goodness and purity in the President's heart. We seek Your continued blessing upon him in all his dealings and relationships so that *never* will he fail You by dishonesty or lying. Safeguard him zealously from the devil, Lord. In Your holy name I pray.

My Concerns Today

_____
_____
_____
_____

My Concerns Today

_____
_____
_____
_____

Nehemiah 9:32

And now, O great and awesome God, You who keep Your promises of love and kindness – do not let all the hardships we have gone through become as nothing.

Prayer

Dear Lord, You know the anguish of the citizens of this country during the past. You know the sorrows, the heartaches, and the confusion of our people. Therefore, I pray that you will give the President divine guidance in leading our people into a better moral and social life. In Christ's name.

Mark 10:27

Without God it is utterly impossible. But with God everything is possible.

Prayer

Dear Lord, as I pray for our President this day I ask You to send complete peace to his spirit and renewed energy to his mind that he may do Your will. Help him to sift through prayerfully and carefully all the exchange of thoughts he has experienced in the last few days. May our nation stand for and do only that which is honorable and righteous in Your sight. In Christ's name I pray.

My Concerns Today

_____

_____

_____

_____

My Concerns Today

_____

_____

_____

_____

2 Corinthians 6:8

We stand true to the Lord, whether others honor us or despise us, whether they criticize us or commend us.

Prayer

Dear Lord, I know there must be hours when the President feels the loneliness of standing for his conviction against the pressure of criticism. Strengthen him with a renewed sense of Your Presence. There must be times, O Lord, when his heart aches from the pain of misunderstanding of others as to his true purposes. Please Lord, bless that pain as You relieve it and transform it into divine empathy for the pain of others. In Christ's name.

2 Corinthians 5:18

All these new things are from God, Who brought us back to Himself through what Christ Jesus did. And God has given us the privilege of urging everyone to come into His favor and be reconciled to Him.

Prayer

Dear Father God, we thank You for this new time – spring with all its beauty – representing to us the resurrection from death into new life. Thank You for the President and this season in the White House. Bless his family as they all renew the consecration of their lives to our Lord Jesus Christ. In His name I pray.

My Concerns Today

_____

_____

_____

_____

My Concerns Today

_____

_____

_____

_____

April 7

2 Corinthians 6:3

We try to live in such a way that no one will ever be offended or kept back from finding the Lord by the way we act, so that no one can find fault with us and blame it on the Lord.

Prayer

Dear Lord, may the Holy Spirit guide the President in his behavior, words and attitudes, that they may always represent Your Spirit flowing through him. I pray that no one will be turned away from Your Presence by anything he does or says. Help him to please You, to serve You, and to honor Your holy name. So bless him, I beseech You. In Christ's name.

April 8

1 Kings 4:29

God gave Solomon great wisdom and understanding, and a mind with broad interests.

Prayer

Dear Lord, we pray that the President will ask God for wisdom and understanding. We know that understanding is one of the great qualities of the spirit. We know it is a reward of deep thinking, right living, and empathy. We know that with understanding comes tolerance and gracious behavior toward others. All these treasures of the spirit we beseech You to produce in the President.

My Concerns Today

_____
_____
_____
_____

My Concerns Today

_____
_____
_____
_____

2 Corinthians 6:14,16

How can light live with darkness? And what union can there be between God's temple and idols? For you are God's temple, the home of the living God, and God has said of you, "I will live in them and walk among them, and I will be their God and they shall be My people."

Prayer

Dear Lord, I know You want all people to become Your people and so I beseech You to guide the President in his talks with and dealings with other leaders who do not, as a nation, acknowledge You as Lord and God. Use him as Your ambassador to the furtherance of Your will being done on earth. In Christ's name I pray.

1 Corinthians 12:27

All of you together are the one body of Christ and each one of you is a separate and necessary part of it.

Prayer

Dear Father God, thank You for Your divine plan of making each of us saved through Christ as a part of the body of Christ. I praise You for the spirit of Christ in the President. During this season, I pray for Your blessed Presence in his life to be especially felt by him. I pray he may not fail You or the Lord Jesus Christ, his Savior, as he fulfills his duties as a part of the body of Christ.

My Concerns Today

_____
_____
_____
_____

My Concerns Today

_____
_____
_____
_____

Isaiah 11:2

And the Spirit of the Lord shall rest upon him, the Spirit of wisdom, understanding, counsel, and might: the Spirit of knowledge and of the fear of the Lord.

Prayer

Dear Father in heaven, Jesus promised that as He and You are one so could we His followers be one with the Father. Therefore, O Lord, for the President, this day I pray that You will bless him with special Oneness with our Lord and Savior. Fill him with wisdom, understanding, and love.

Psalm 55:22

Give your burdens to the Lord. He will carry them. He will not permit the godly to slip or fall.

Prayer

Dear Lord, the President needs You. He needs to cast his burdens upon You. Responsibilities concerning relationships with so many other nations may be heavy upon him now, O Lord. Hear my prayer for this brave and humble man, our leader. Let him neither slip nor fall in the administration of his office and the fulfilling of his duties. In Christ's name I pray.

My Concerns Today

_____

_____

_____

_____

My Concerns Today

_____

_____

_____

_____

Psalm 61:5

For You have heard my vows, O God, to praise You every day, and You have given me the blessings You reserve for those who reverence Your name.

Prayer

Dear Father God, I praise Your holy name that the President has vowed to love and obey You. I beseech Your continued blessings upon him. You have promised blessings and even miracles to those who reverence Your name and follow Your Son, our Lord. In His name I pray.

John 15:21,24

The people of the world will persecute you because you belong to Me, for they do not know God who sent Me....But, I will send you the Comforter, the Holy Spirit, the Source of all truth.

Prayer

Dear Lord Jesus, thank You for telling Your followers that they would be persecuted. We realize the President will be persecuted by those who do not know God, but we praise Your holy name for sending the Comforter to guide and direct him. In Your blessed name and for Your glory I pray.

My Concerns Today

_____
_____
_____
_____

My Concerns Today

_____
_____
_____
_____

Psalm 60:1,4-5

Lord, restore us again to Your favor; You have given us a banner to rally to; all who love truth will rally to it; then You can deliver Your beloved people.

Prayer

Dear Lord, our country and the President need Your help. We ask for that help. I pray now in spirit with all who pray daily for him in these times of turmoil and concern. Open every mind and heart in America, O Lord, to the importance and consequences of decisions to be made. In Christ's name.

Psalm 22:25

Yes, I will stand and praise You before all the people. I will publicly fulfill my vows in the presence of all who reverence Your name.

Prayer

Dear Lord, thank You for providing our country with a President who honors You and stands before people in praise of You and Your holiness. I beseech You to enable the President to fulfill, in faithful service, every vow he has made. In accordance to Your guidance through the Holy Spirit, may he be the leader You want him to be.

My Concerns Today

_____
_____
_____
_____

My Concerns Today

_____
_____
_____
_____

2 Chronicles 1:10

Now give me wisdom and knowledge to rule them properly, for who is able to govern by himself such a great nation as this one of Yours?

Prayer

Dear Lord God, may the President seek You this day for wisdom and understanding. I, this day, join him in spirit in that prayer. Our nation is a mighty nation and a great nation in many ways. But I beseech You to make our nation spiritually greater under the leadership of this President than it has ever been. In Christ's name.

2 Chronicles 7:14

If My people…will humble themselves and pray and search for Me, and turn from their wicked ways, I will hear them from heaven and forgive their sins, and heal their land.

Prayer

Dear Lord God, just as You required humility and prayer and contrite hearts of the Israelites, so today You demand of us the same. I pray that our people will humble themselves before You. As we look to the President for leadership, we shall as one nation unite in spirit to receive Your guidance and obey Your will.

My Concerns Today

_____
_____
_____
_____

My Concerns Today

_____
_____
_____
_____

Proverbs 18:15

The intelligent man is always open to new ideas. In fact, he looks for them.

Prayer

Dear Father God, I believe the President is an intelligent man, open in mind and spirit to new ideas. Please, dear Father, keep him that way. Then he will always be looking for new ideas regarding the preservation of peace and the solution to unemployment in our nation. Guide him in new ways to bring about a decrease in crime among our people and to improve our relationships with other governments. In Christ's name.

Psalm 15:6

Let everything alive give praise to the Lord: You praise Him!

Prayer

Oh Almighty God in heaven, Maker and Ruler of all the universe, I join the President and all members of the human race who praise You this day. Give the President boldness to stand before this nation of people as a constant witness of one who praises You, Holy God. You made us and redeemed us through Christ. In His name we pour out our praises and gratitude to You.

My Concerns Today

_____
_____
_____
_____

My Concerns Today

_____
_____
_____
_____

Proverbs 8:16

Rulers rule well with help.

Prayer

Dear Lord, we do not think of the President as a ruler, but as a leader and coworker. However, we know from Your Holy Word that the position of ruler of long ago days was similar in responsibility to the position of leadership in our day. Therefore, I now implore Your help for every problem for which the President must seek a solution. In Christ's name I pray.

Proverbs 10:31

The good man gives wise advice, but the liar's counsel is shunned.

Prayer

Dear Lord, I pray that the President will always carefully consider all counsel offered him. The President should seek counsel and advice from good men in our government, but be wise in rejecting counsel he cannot endorse. In the love of Christ, we pray for this President. In the name of Jesus Christ.

My Concerns Today

_____

_____

_____

_____

My Concerns Today

_____

_____

_____

_____

Proverbs 28:2

When there is moral rot within a nation, its government topples easily; but with honest, sensible leaders there is stability.

Prayer

Dear Father, we thank You again for the President. We pray that always he will be an honest man, a sensible leader, giving our people the stability the United States has always exemplified. We praise You for guidance of our Founding Fathers, and for the documents which guide our leaders. As we rely upon Your direction, O God, we experience stability even during transfer of power. Therefore, during these first months in office, we pray for him.

Proverbs 28:5

Evil men do not understand the importance of justice, but those who follow the Lord are much concerned about it.

Prayer

Dear Heavenly Father, just and holy God, who loves men of justice, bless the President this day and every day as he continues his efforts toward justice for all people. It is no doubt practically impossible for every law and regulation to be equally fair for all people. But we are aware of how Your Spirit is seeking fairness for all. Bless the President in every effort. I pray in Christ's name.

My Concerns Today

_____
_____
_____
_____

My Concerns Today

_____
_____
_____
_____

Proverbs 14:26

Reverence for God gives a man deep strength.

Prayer

Dear Father in heaven, thank You for a President who reverences You, the Almighty and Everlasting God. You are the source of the President's strength as indeed You are the Source of strength for all believers. Bless him with adequate and renewed strength this day as he continues to search for Your truth and to bless this country through his leadership.

Proverbs 14:29-30

A wise man controls his temper. He knows that anger causes mistakes. A relaxed attitude lengthens a man's life.

Prayer

Dear Father in heaven, we thank You for the marvelous self-control and relaxed attitude which the President constantly displays. We pray that day by day in every situation – with heads of state to the humblest of servants – our Christian President shall maintain complete control of himself. We have seen it thus far – magnificent control – and for this, we give You, the Source of such control our deepest expression of gratitude. In Christ's name.

My Concerns Today

_____
_____
_____
_____

My Concerns Today

_____
_____
_____
_____

Proverbs 15:31-32

If you profit from constructive criticism, you will be elected to the wise men's hall of fame. But to reject criticism is to harm yourself and your own best interests.

Prayer

Dear Lord, we beseech You to look in favor upon the President, who does take criticism and benefit from it. We pray that You permit only the criticism that is profitable for him and his programs. I pray thus, most Holy God, that this criticism he must deal with will be in the best interests not only of this man, but of the nation as a whole. We thank You for his devoted service. In Christ's name.

Proverbs 16:11

The Lord demands fairness in every business deal.

Prayer

Dear Lord, we see and hear the President speak constantly of fairness to all the people or corporations involved. We praise You for this – that Your Spirit is actively evident in this man's thinking and in his speech. Please keep it so as he and other leaders work on the various programs of government. Bless him as he now considers the requests and needs of the various peoples of other nations. May he ever be Your spokesman and messenger delivering to the minds of the various leaders Your will for them that world's people may live in peace.

My Concerns Today

_____

_____

_____

_____

My Concerns Today

_____

_____

_____

_____

Romans 8:28

And we know that all that happens to us is working for our good if we love God and are fitting into His plans.

Prayer

Dear Lord, I thank You for the good that has happened in the life of the President. Thank you, Lord, that by loving You we see that all things fit into Your divine plan. Keep our President always aware that You are Sovereign. May he ever seek Your divine guidance. Bless him as he fits himself in service according to Your plans.

My Concerns Today

_____
_____
_____
_____

Isaiah 26:3

He will keep in perfect peace all those who trust in Him, whose thoughts turn often to the Lord.

Prayer

Dear Father God, as the Christian people of our country turn their thoughts to You in prayer, we especially pray for Your peace to descend upon our nation. In times of peace man should seek the spread of spiritual development in order to undertake the solving of the problems of material and social progress. So with faith in Your Almighty Power, bless the President as he and our people work together for progress not only for America but for the world.

My Concerns Today

_____
_____
_____
_____

Proverbs 16:3

Commit your work to the Lord, then it will succeed.

Prayer

Dear Father God, I praise Your Holy Name. I thank You for the countless blessings You have bestowed upon me. I praise You and thank You for the life and work of the President, and beseech Your special blessing upon him as he applies his mind to the problems of the country. His work with others must succeed for the salvation of body, mind, and spirit of the poor in our country. Lead him, O Lord. In Your blessed name I pray.

Philippians 3:12

I haven't learned all I should even yet, but I keep working toward that day when I will finally be all that Christ saved me for and wants me to be.

Prayer

Dear Lord God, I thank You for the President, who day by day is walking the path of obedience, self-discipline, and constructive leadership. I pray he seeks Your will in his deliberations and in his actions and keeps working toward the goals of national welfare and of personal spiritual development. Bless him, dear Lord, with constant growth and achievement. In Your blessed name I pray.

My Concerns Today

_____

_____

_____

_____

My Concerns Today

_____

_____

_____

_____

Proverbs 19:20,27

Get all the advice you can and be wise the rest of your life....Stop listening to teaching that contradicts what you know is right.

Prayer

Dear Lord, the President needs to receive advice and counsel from many people because our nation is so big and life is so complicated. Bless him as he considers the advice he receives. Help him, dear Lord, to turn a deaf ear to any ideas or philosophies which are not right in the sight of God and are not authenticated by Your Holy Word. I pray for this President to be a student of Your Word. Guide him, O Lord, for I pray in the name of Jesus Christ.

My Concerns Today

_____

_____

_____

_____

Psalm 5:8-9

Lord, lead me as You promised You would... Tell me clearly what to do, which way to turn.

Prayer

Dear Lord, as You have promised in Your Holy Word, lead the President clearly in his negotiations. As he confers with heads of state and officials of other countries, show him in every circumstance which way he should turn. Tell him clearly what to say in each deliberation and conference. In Christ's name and for the good of the whole world we pray this prayer.

My Concerns Today

_____

_____

_____

_____

Psalm 16:7

I will bless the Lord who counsels me; He gives me wisdom in the night. He tells me what to do.

Prayer

Dear Lord, as the President travels and confers on matters of importance to all people, bless him richly. Let him feel Your presence and guidance in such a sure and strong way that he shall talk and act with the confidence of those who walk with You, our God, and in the Spirit of our Lord Jesus Christ. In His name I now pray.

Psalm 22:28-29

For the Lord is King and rules the nations. Both proud and humble together, all who are mortal – born to die – shall worship Him.

Prayer

Dear Father God, we are so happy that the President travels and speaks to the proud and the humble, the rich and the poor. When he stands before them, a simple and humble man, yet occupying the greatest office in the world, he represents You, the God so many worship. Thank You in Christ's name for his daily witness.

My Concerns Today

_____

_____

_____

_____

My Concerns Today

_____

_____

_____

_____

Isaiah 42:1,6

I have put My Spirit upon him; he will reveal justice to the nations of the world....I, the Lord, have called you to demonstrate My righteousness. I will guard and support you. You shall also be a light to guide the nations unto Me.

Prayer

Dear Father God, as the President moves about among the people and confers with the leaders of other nations, I pray for Your Spirit to be in him and in perfect control of his speech and actions. Praise to You O Most Holy God, for lifting up Your servant for our leader. In Christ's name.

Daniel 9:17

O our God, hear Your servant's prayer. Listen as I plead.

Prayer

Dear Lord God, we believe that during these busy days, the President is constantly seeking Your presence. Bless him and guide his every word in the many deliberations of State. Bless each person with whom he confers, for we pray that Your Holy Will shall be done by these leaders. Strengthen through Your Holy Spirit the prayer power of our people in support of our leaders. In Christ's name.

My Concerns Today

_____
_____
_____
_____

My Concerns Today

_____
_____
_____
_____

May 9

Psalm 66:3

How awe-inspiring are Your deeds, O God! How great Your power!

Prayer

Dear Father God, how great indeed is Your power. We praise Your Holiness, as well as Your power. And now we see You at work in the world through the life of the President. We pray this day that every act and word of his will reflect Your Spirit. Prepare, O Lord, the minds of those with whom he confers to see Your truth in what he says so that all of the nations may work toward peace.

May 10

Matthew 5:9

Happy are those who strive for peace – they shall be called Sons of God.

Prayer

Dear Heavenly Father, as You see the President striving for peace among the nations, bless him, O Lord, with sensitivity and compassion for all. Enhance his sincerity, enlarge his vision, strengthen his will and keep firm his determination to the end, that Your will may be done through him for all mankind. In Christ's name.

My Concerns Today

_____
_____
_____
_____

My Concerns Today

_____
_____
_____
_____

Proverbs 20:24

Since the Lord is directing our steps, why try to understand everything that happens along the way?

Prayer

Dear Lord, thank You for directing the President daily – indeed hour by hour – or moment by moment, as he meets with many leaders. You have been so faithful in Your protection and leadership. May he reveal the Spirit of Jesus Christ by manner and word. For all Your blessings, we thank You. Now as he works on national and international affairs, we beseech Your continued blessing and guidance. In Christ's name I pray.

My Concerns Today

_____

_____

_____

_____

Proverbs 21:2

We can justify our every deed, but God looks at our motives. God is more pleased when we are just and fair than when we give Him gifts.

Prayer

Dear Father, the President is a man I believe of high and noble thought, of pure and holy motive, striving to be just and fair to all men of every race and nation. Humbly we beseech You to look upon this man with mercy. Daily he needs You, O Lord. Hide not Your countenance from him. Sustain him in bodily strength, increase the keenness of his mind and ennoble his spirit.

My Concerns Today

_____

_____

_____

_____

John 14:13

You can ask Him for anything, using My name, and I will do it, for this will bring praise to the Father because of what I, the Son, will do for you.

Prayer

Dear Lord God, in the name of our blessed Savior, Jesus, I beseech You to bless the President. I pray that he will turn his mind and heart to You each day and the requests made by him in Jesus' name will be honored with answers from You. Those answers will be beneficial to all concerned. You have promised we can ask anything in Christ's name and it will be done bringing praise to Your own holy self.

My Concerns Today

_____
_____
_____
_____

John 15:8

My true disciples produce bountiful harvests. This brings great glory to My Father.

Prayer

Dear Lord God, Your true disciples do produce bountiful harvests and we trust that the President is doing just that. Bless him abundantly, O Lord. May bountiful harvests of prosperity, peace, understanding, and progress resound to his credit and to the well-being and happiness of the citizens he serves in Your name and to Your glory. In Jesus Christ's name I pray.

My Concerns Today

_____
_____
_____
_____

Revelation 2:26

To everyone who overcomes — who to the very end keeps on doing things that please Me — I will give power over the nations.

Prayer

Dear Lord, bless the President with power to persuade nations to come to terms with their enemies in order that peace may come about. Give the President courage and wisdom as he seeks to bring warring nations into a permanent agreement. In Christ's name.

Revelation 3:20

Look! I have been standing at the door and I am constantly knocking. If anyone hears Me calling him and opens the door, I will come in and fellowship with him and he with Me.

Prayer

Dear Lord, thank You for giving this precious promise of fellowship to all who open the door. The President has long ago opened the door to You, his Savior, and invited You into his heart and mind to fellowship with him. Bless him, O Lord, with Your constant Presence. Give him Your special visions, O Lord, as You have done for Your chosen ones through the ages. In Christ's name I pray.

My Concerns Today

_____
_____
_____
_____

My Concerns Today

_____
_____
_____
_____

May 17

Nehemiah 9:13-14

You came down from Mount Sinai and spoke with them from heaven and gave them good laws and true commands, including the laws about the Holy Sabbath.

Prayer

Dear Lord, I pray that the President will be so impressed by Your Holy Spirit regarding the sin of our people in their failure to keep the Sabbath day holy that he will call our people to account. If stores and markets were closed on Sunday, massive amounts of energy would be conserved. Let him speak now, O Lord, regarding the "keeping of the Sabbath." In Christ's name I pray.

May 18

Ezekiel 44:24

Their decisions must be based upon My laws. And the priests themselves shall obey My rules and regulations at all the sacred festivals and they shall see to it that the Sabbath is kept a sacred day.

Prayer

Dear Lord, if among our national leaders there are rebellious spirits, deal with them this day I pray. For among our national leaders there needs to be a union of spirit regarding our worship of You as the true and living God – the Creator of the universe – yet the Father God of our nation. Lead the President in calling our people back to keeping the Sabbath a holy day for Christ's glory.

My Concerns Today

_____
_____
_____
_____

My Concerns Today

_____
_____
_____
_____

Hosea 6:3

Oh, that we might know the Lord! Let us press on to know Him, and He will respond to us as surely as the coming of dawn or the rain of early spring.

Prayer

Dear Lord, we do want to know You. I pray that our President wants to know You more and more. May he know You as his Savior, as his Creator, as his God and Father. He needs to know Your mind and Your will through the presence and guidance of Your Holy Spirit. Bless him with that wisdom and guidance in the dealings with leaders of other nations, so that Your holy will may be done on earth. We praise You through Jesus Christ.

Jeremiah 32:27

I am the Lord, the God of all mankind; is there anything too hard for Me?

Prayer

Dear Lord, all of us who love You acknowledge You as Lord and Savior, as God of all mankind, and know that nothing is too hard for You. We praise You. We believe You want peace for Your people in all parts of the world. But especially at this time the President and his coworkers in foreign affairs need a miracle performed by Your Holy Spirit to bring about negotiations for peace in the Middle East. Hear the fervent prayers of Your people in Christ's name.

My Concerns Today

_____
_____
_____
_____

My Concerns Today

_____
_____
_____
_____

May 21

Hebrews 2:20; 3:6

The Lord is in His holy temple; let all the earth be silent before Him. His power is just the same as always.

Prayer

Dear Lord, praises be unto You. You are in Your Holy Place – ruler of all the universe. Your power is the same today as it has always been. Therefore my soul bows before You with this request to give to the President a holiness of purpose and keenness of mind as he searches with others the secrets You have hidden in the earth. If Your people of future generations are to survive, reveal Your secrets of energy before it is too late. In Christ's name I pray.

My Concerns Today

_____
_____
_____
_____

May 22

Proverbs 4:11-12

I would have you learn this great fact! that a life of doing right is the wisest life there is. If you live that kind of life, you will not limp or stumble as you run.

Prayer

Dear Lord God, we believe that to do right is what the President wants. He has set his mind and heart upon this course. He has acknowledged You as his Creator and Savior. Therefore now we pray that You will take his trained mind and humble spirit and by Your divine Spirit lead him into daily acts of good and wise leadership for our nation and for the world. In Christ's name I pray.

My Concerns Today

_____
_____
_____
_____

May 23

Exodus 6:7-8

I will accept them as My people and be their God. I will bring them into the land I promised to give to Abraham, Isaac, and Jacob. It shall belong to My people.

Prayer

Dear Lord, Your mighty power I acknowledge. Your word I reverence. Your will for each nation is beyond my understanding. Nevertheless, at this time in history, we believe that the Hebrew people are Yours. To them You have made unbreakable promises. You work in ways unknown to man, so as I pray for the President, I implore You to step into the Middle East situation and work a miracle for peace.

May 24

Psalm 145:17-18

The Lord is fair in everything He does, and full of kindness. He is close to all who call on Him sincerely.

Prayer

Dear Lord God, we know You are a good God, a loving Father, and a constant worker of miracles. Since it is Your good pleasure to work miracles and to surprise Your sons of earth, I pray this day for a special blessing of miracles every day to help the President to bear the burdens of his highly responsible office. All foreign and national problems with which he deals need Your divine touch of power for their correct solution. For Your divine touch I pray.

My Concerns Today

_____
_____
_____
_____

My Concerns Today

_____
_____
_____
_____

May 25

Isaiah 24:20

The world staggers like a drunkard; it shakes like a tent in a storm. It falls and will not rise again, for the sins of this earth are very great.

Prayer

Dear Lord, we know that sins destroy. Your Holy Spirit has taught the President that You are a Holy God and cannot look upon sin. We pray, O Lord that the President and all members of his family may stand for morality in every phase of life. Bless them. Guard and strengthen them and uphold them as Your witnesses in high places and with people who hold high offices, that You may be glorified. In Christ's name I pray.

May 26

Romans 8:14,16

For all who are led by the Spirit of God are sons of God. For His Holy Spirit speaks to us deep in our hearts, and tells us that we really are God's children.

Prayer

Dear Lord Jesus, Your servant Paul has taught us that we are sons of God along with You, our Savior, and joint heirs with You in His glory. But because we, along with the President, are heirs of God to share in His glory, we must share in Your suffering. Bless the President, O Lord, as he shares in the suffering of God to get problems solved and bring peace to the nations. In Your blessed name.

My Concerns Today

_____
_____
_____
_____

My Concerns Today

_____
_____
_____
_____

Galatians 5:25

If we are living now by the Holy Spirit's power, let us follow the Holy Spirit's leading in every part of our lives.

Prayer

Dear Lord God, many times the President has major international problems before him. He needs the guidance of the Holy Spirit to give him definite and decisive leadership in international problems. We beseech You, our Father, to empower the President with the divine leadership to solve these problems. Send Your Spirit, O Lord, into the mind and heart of other national leaders and bring about in them Your holy will. In Christ's name I pray.

Psalm 36:5-6

Your steadfast love, O Lord, is as great as all the heavens. Your faithfulness reaches beyond the clouds. Your justice is as solid as God's mountains. Your decisions are full of wisdom as the oceans are with water.

Prayer

Dear Lord God, we are counting on Your faithfulness in ministering to the needs of the President as he works with our Congress on the major problems of the nation. I pray that all our government officials who know You as their God will turn their minds and hearts toward You. May they be fulfilled with Your Holy Spirit to guide their thinking, sharpen their minds, and flood their spirits with the desire to do Your will.

My Concerns Today

_____
_____
_____
_____

My Concerns Today

_____
_____
_____
_____

May 29

Psalm 58: 10-11

The godly shall rejoice in the triumph of right…At last everyone will know that good is rewarded, and that there is a God who judges justly here on earth.

Prayer

Dear Lord God, we know You love righteousness and hate evil. We know You bless the godly who seek You and Your Truth. Therefore we pray that the good which is found in the President and every official of government who works with him will be rewarded by You for the ultimate good of our nation and other peoples of the world. We pray for peace among the nations, O God. In Christ's name.

May 30

Daniel 10:19

"God loves you very much," he said, "Don't be afraid! Calm yourself; be strong…yes, strong!"

Prayer

Dear Lord, I thank You that You will constantly speak reassuring words to your President. You speak to his mind and spirit because You love him. You counsel with him because You wish to give guidance and clarity to his thinking. Encourage and inspire him to keep his spirit calm and strong even in the midst of turmoil. For Your goodness to him, I praise Your holy name.

My Concerns Today

_____
_____
_____
_____

My Concerns Today

_____
_____
_____
_____

1 John 4:21

And God Himself has said that one must love not only God, but his brother, too.

Prayer

Dear Lord, as I pray for the President to follow Your guidance, I pray that Your love may constantly be reflected in his life. May he send out, as Dr. Laubach taught us, flash-prayers of love even for his enemies. Let Your love be released and work its miracles of healing and brotherhood among the nations. In Christ's name I pray.

My Concerns Today

_____

_____

_____

_____

June 1

Genesis 2:3

And God blessed the seventh day and declared it holy, because it was the day when He ceased this work of creation.

Prayer

Dear Lord God, thank You for a President who loves You and obeys Your commandment to keep the Sabbath day holy. Help the President, O Lord, wield a mighty influence in our country for people to return to a national observance of You, our God, each Sabbath day. If You, the Creator, rested on the seventh day, surely man should set aside one day to worship You. In Christ's name I pray.

June 2

Deuteronomy 6:25

For it always goes well with us when we obey all the laws of the Lord our God.

Prayer

Dear Father God, bless the President with an honest mind. May Your Holy Spirit quicken in his mind each problem he faces with the ultimate and most important questions: What decision does this problem demand of me and the American people, and what decision will be in obedience to the laws of God? How can we help other nations and yet not interfere? What is Your law, O God, to guide us in this need? O Lord, help the President as he seeks Your guidance and then open the doors which allow him to follow it.

My Concerns Today

_____
_____
_____
_____

My Concerns Today

_____
_____
_____
_____

Exodus 20:8-9

Remember to observe the Sabbath as a holy day. Six days a week for your daily duties and your regular work, but the seventh day is a day of Sabbath rest before the Lord, your God.

Prayer

Dear Lord, help the President stand boldly for the Sabbath day to be kept holy. If places of business were closed on Sunday, more and more people of our country would be led to worship You and rest physically. By such obedience to Your laws and cooperative effort our people would conserve much energy. In Christ's name I pray.

Psalm 9:7-8,10

The Lord lives on forever; He sits upon His throne to judge justly the nations of the world. All those who know Your mercy, Lord, will count on You for help. For You have never yet forsaken those who trust in You.

Prayer

Dear Lord, as the President visits with and communicates with people of other nations, may he have Your blessings of guidance and protection. May his visits reveal his complete trust in Your love, Your grace and Your power that he may be a symbol to all nations of one who trusts in You.

My Concerns Today

_____

_____

_____

_____

My Concerns Today

_____

_____

_____

_____

June 5

1 John 4:6

But we are children of God; that is why only those who have walked and talked with God will listen to us.

Prayer

Dear Lord God, protect, we pray, any representative of the President sent to other nations. Those who do not approve of our President and his stand on human rights might seek to do that person harm, but we know You will send attending angels to protect that representative. It has to be as Your Word said, those only who walk and talk with You will listen to those who fight for human rights. We thank You for Your protection of our President. In Christ's name.

June 6

1 John 4:15

Anyone who believes and says that Jesus is the Son of God has God living in him, and he is living with God.

Prayer

Dear Lord God, we acknowledge Jesus as Your Son, and our President acknowledges Him before the whole world. Therefore, we pray as You live in him and his family that through their words of love and goodwill for all people Your Holy Spirit will take control of other lands. We pray that Your Spirit of love and cooperation could quell hate and discord and bind the nations together in love.

My Concerns Today

_____

_____

_____

_____

My Concerns Today

_____

_____

_____

_____

June 7

Jeremiah 17:7

Blessed is the man who trusts in the Lord and has made the Lord his hope and confidence.

Prayer

Dear Lord God, we thank You for the President, who is trusting in You and Your Holy Word, his confidence and hope. He is strengthened for his great responsibilities by Your grace and compassion. He is guided and directed by Your Holy Spirit. Continue, O Lord, Your constant blessings of strength, guidance, grace, and mercy unto him and all his family. In Jesus Christ's blessed name I pray.

June 8

Jeremiah 17:10

He, the Lord, searches all hearts and examines deepest motives so He can give to each person his right reward, according to his deeds.

Prayer

Dear Lord God, we know that through Your grace and the love and sacrifice of our Savior we have the promise of salvation. But also we are deeply aware of our obligation, responsibility and privilege as followers of the Lord Jesus Christ, that our hearts must be pure as we live, work and serve You. Therefore, we beseech Your blessing on the President as he seeks to serve his fellow man in Your blessed Name. In Christ's name.

My Concerns Today

_____
_____
_____
_____

My Concerns Today

_____
_____
_____
_____

Jeremiah 18:9-10

If I announce that I will make a certain nation strong and great, but then that nation changes its mind and turns evil and refuses to obey Me, then I too will change My mind and not bless that nation as I had said I would.

Prayer

Dear Lord God, throughout the history of our country You have spoken to the hearts of many to tell them that our nation should be strong and great. But in many ways our sins are on the increase as revealed through statistics. We have dishonored You and disobeyed Your laws. Please, O Lord, bless the President and his influence for morality in our national life.

Jeremiah 22:8-9

"Why did the Lord do it? Why did He destroy such a great city?" And the answer will be, "Because the people living here forgot the Lord their God and violated His agreement with them, for they worshiped idols."

Prayer

Dear Lord God, forgive the people of America for worshiping the idols of materialism, sex and violence and forgetting the promises of trust in You, the true God. During this administration of the President, may a great wave of true repentance sweep across our country with a turning of our people back to the true virtues upheld by our founding fathers and to a reverent worship of You. In Christ's name.

My Concerns Today

_____

_____

_____

My Concerns Today

_____

_____

_____

Ephesians 1:19

I pray that you will begin to understand how incredibly great His power is to help those who believe Him.

Prayer

Dear Lord God, Father of us all, in the name of Your Son, our Savior I pray that the President will consistently grow in understanding of Your great and unlimited power to guide him, strengthen him, and enlighten him. Help us all, Lord, to know that You enlighten people of all races through Your Holy Spirit. We believe our universe is under Your control. In Christ's name I pray.

Ephesians 3:20

Glory be to God, who by His mighty power at work within us is able to do far more than we would ever dare to ask or even dream of- infinitely beyond our highest prayers, desires, thoughts or hopes.

Prayer

Dear Lord God, as I pray for the President and for each official of our government, may Your Spirit be at work in them. You will do far more for our nation and for the world than we ask or dream of. Therefore, in humility and in trust, I lift up to Your throne of grace the actions and deeds of our national leaders.

My Concerns Today

_____

_____

_____

_____

My Concerns Today

_____

_____

_____

_____

June 13

Psalm 37:39

The Lord saves the godly! He is their salvation and their refuge when trouble comes.

Prayer

Dear Lord God, how we praise You that the psalms of praise and thanksgiving have been preserved through the ages for our benefit. The President is a godly man. Trouble will come upon him as it comes to all of us, but because of his great responsibilities, many, varied and more serious troubles will assail him. I beseech You, most glorious Lord, to be known by him as his constant refuge. In Christ's name.

June 14

Jeremiah 4:2

If you will swear by Me alone, the living God, and begin to live good, honest, clean lives, then you will be a testimony to the nations of the world and they will come to Me and glorify My name.

Prayer

Dear Lord God, thank you for the President. May our First Family always represent You, the living God, so that all people of other nations may be drawn to You when they think of our First Family. In Christ's name I pray.

My Concerns Today

_____
_____
_____
_____

My Concerns Today

_____
_____
_____
_____

June 15

Jeremiah 5:5

I will go now to their leaders, the man of importance, and speak to them, for they know the ways of the Lord and the judgment that follows sin.

Prayer

Dear Lord God, for the President and for every member of Congress we this day pray Your most profound blessings of astuteness, wisdom, and integrity in their deliberations regarding the energy needs of the nation. The earth, sea and sky are under Your control, but man needs Your wisdom and guidance in finding, developing and using the sources of energy You have created. Please help our leaders, O Lord.

June 16

Deuteronomy 8: 11-14

Beware that in your plenty you don't forget the Lord your God and begin to disobey Him. For when you have become full and prosperous and have built fine homes to live in—that is the time to watch out that you don't become proud and forget the Lord your God.

Prayer

Dear Father God, You have blessed us with great plenty in America, yet in our affluence and worldly success we have often forgotten You. As I pray for the President and other government officials today, I also pray for the citizens of our country to turn away from the worship of material things to the worship of You, our God and Redeemer. In Christ's name I pray.

My Concerns Today

_____
_____
_____
_____

My Concerns Today

_____
_____
_____
_____

Isaiah 26:12

Lord grant us peace; for all we have and are has come from You.

Prayer

Dear Lord God, Almighty and Everlasting Lord, our Creator and our Redeemer, we magnify and praise Your holy name. In honor and reverence we pray for our country, our leaders, and for the President. We pray, O Lord, that our leaders will truly be statesman and not just politicians. And especially at this moment, we pray that Your grace and mantle of true Christian leadership may fall upon the President that all who deal with him may know that Your Spirit is within him. In Christ's name.

Proverbs 3:12

Do not resent it when God chastens and corrects you, for His punishment is proof of His love. Just as a father punishes a son he delights in, to make him better, so the Lord corrects you.

Prayer

Dear Father, thank You for loving us enough to seek us out even in the midst of our sins, disobedience, neglect of You, or even in our open rebellion, to chasten and correct us. We pray for the proof of Your love in correcting the President when the need should arise. Through the love of Christ who died for us, we pray.

My Concerns Today

_____

_____

_____

_____

My Concerns Today

_____

_____

_____

_____

Proverbs 3:7-8

Don't be conceited, sure of your own wisdom. Instead, trust and reverence the Lord, and turn your back on evil; when you do that, then you will be given renewed health and vitality.

Prayer

Dear Lord, help the President never to be conceited. He needs to be a wise man. May he trust in You, his loving Father and Holy God. Give him wisdom that he may be a natural leader under Your authority. O Lord, may he be always aware that You are the God of all people and Ruler of the universe. No doubt there is no one who knows how much he wants to act under Your authority. Through divine provision meet his every need this day I pray.

Ephesians 4:7

Christ has given each of us special abilities.

Prayer

Dear Lord, You have given the President many gifts. Daily let him ask himself "In planning for others, have I failed to be conscientious? In my dealing with friends have I failed to be sincere? In teaching and admonishing others, have I failed to practice what I teach? In communion with my Lord, have I humbly sought His control that I might receive true guidance from Him?" Daily revitalize Your Holy Spirit's work in the President's life. I pray this in Christ's name.

My Concerns Today

_____
_____
_____
_____

My Concerns Today

_____
_____
_____
_____

June 21

Psalm 119:52

From my earliest youth I have tried to obey You; Your Word has been my comfort.

Prayer

Dear Lord God, from one who loved You so much that beautiful songs of praise spilled from his lips, we receive this message. May it be true of the President. Hear my prayer for him today, dear Father, in the name of Your Son. Guide him and enlighten him. May he trust in You daily.

June 22

Luke 18:27

He (Jesus) replied, "God can do what man can't."

Prayer

Dear Father God, we worship You. We praise and reverence Your holy name. We thank You for our Savior, Jesus Christ. We praise Him and love Him. We know and recognize Your unlimited power operating not only in the whole universe, but in the hearts of man. We know and believe that Your Holy Spirit will do for us that which we cannot do. Therefore I pray that the Holy Spirit will open the hearts and minds of leaders who disagree with the President that together they may come to a mutual understanding of Your holy will.

My Concerns Today

_____

_____

_____

_____

My Concerns Today

_____

_____

_____

_____

June 23

Lamentations 3:21-23

Yet there is one ray of hope: His compassion never ends. It is only the Lord's mercies that have kept us from complete destruction. Great is His faithfulness; His loving kindness begins afresh each day

.

Prayer

Dear Lord, we recognize Your unlimited mercy and divine compassion by which we are so constantly blessed and in Your debt we shall ever be. But because You are our loving Father with unlimited treasure, we beseech for the President the joys of everlasting hope, and complete trust in Your care and guidance along his rugged path of responsibility. In Christ's name I pray.

My Concerns Today

_____

_____

_____

_____

June 24

Luke 6:32-33

Do you think you deserve credit for merely loving those who love you? Even the godless do that. And if you do good only to those who do you good – is that so wonderful? Even sinners do that much.

Prayer

Dear Lord God, thank You for the President. He may often be tempted to fall into the worldly way of loving only where he is loved – of doing good to those who can do something for him. Save him, O Lord, from these temptations so prevalent in our society. Keep him a wise, just, and faithful servant of all people. In Your Son's precious name I pray.

My Concerns Today

_____

_____

_____

_____

Proverbs 11:27-28

If you search for good, you will find God's favor…trust in your money and down you go! Trust in God and flourish as a tree!

Prayer

Dear Lord God, thank You for the President's search for good. May it always be a lifelong search for that good which comes only from You. May he never put his trust in money or the material things of life. May his mind and heart be set on the spiritual elements of life. Bless and help him in his concern for human rights and give him Your guidance in all his efforts. May he do Your holy will. In the name of Jesus Christ I pray.

2 Corinthians 7:1

Let us turn away from every thing wrong, whether of body or spirit, and purify ourselves, living in the wholesome fear of God, giving ourselves to Him alone.

Prayer

Dear Lord God, may the President turn to You for the accomplishment of Your will in this troubled world. In this confused society with its many complexities bless the President, O Lord, with Your Spirit. May Your Holy Spirit give him the gift of discernment in every problem, large or small, as he devotes his mind and heart to the leadership of our nation. In Christ's name I pray.

My Concerns Today

_____
_____
_____
_____

My Concerns Today

_____
_____
_____
_____

2 Corinthians 8:11

Having started the ball rolling so enthusiastically, you should carry this project through to completion just as gladly, giving whatever you can out of whatever you have.

Prayer

Dear Lord God, bless the President that he may have the spirit of giving with a glad heart. May his generosity be an inspiration to the citizens of the country to give joyously and graciously. May we all learn to give as Your Word has taught us, to share from our abundance to meet the needs of others.

2 Corinthians 9:13-14

Those you help will be glad, not only because of your generous gifts to themselves and others, but they will praise God for this proof that your deeds are as good as your doctrine. And they will pray for you with deep fervor and feeling because of the wonderful grace of God shown through you.

Prayer

Dear Lord, thank You that as our President spends time with Your Word You will increase his spirit of giving. By his example of generosity he will inspire other officials. Thereby, You, Lord, will magnify gracious living in our country among our leadership. May Your Spirit of giving permeate our land.

My Concerns Today

_____
_____
_____
_____

My Concerns Today

_____
_____
_____
_____

June 29

Hebrews 6:18

He has given us both His promise and His oath, two things we can completely count on, for it is impossible for God to tell a lie.

Prayer

Dear Lord God, we know it is impossible for You to tell a lie or break a promise. Therefore, as I pray daily for the President I am praying with confidence that You will so guide him and strengthen him that he will be able to deal with leaders of other nations to the greatest ultimate benefit for all. I am trusting Your work being done through him. In Your Son's name I pray.

June 30

Matthew 10:18

You must stand trial before governors and kings for My sake. This will give you the opportunity to tell them about Me, yes, to witness to the world.

Prayer

Dear Lord God, You have brought many of Your followers to testing places where they stood before governors and kings. And You upheld them – pouring into them Your power. Now I ask that as the President stands before those in authority from other lands that Your Spirit of power and grace be his sustaining strength. In Christ's name I pray.

My Concerns Today

_____
_____
_____
_____

My Concerns Today

_____
_____
_____
_____

Psalm 67:2

Send us around the world with the news of Your saving power and Your eternal plan for all mankind.

Prayer

Dear Lord God, You have raised up leaders throughout the ages who were chosen to deliver Your messages to the people. We pray for our President to be one of those leaders. Choose others, Lord God, from our nation to be messengers for You. In Christ's name I pray.

Proverbs 22:12

The Lord preserves the upright, but ruins the plans of the wicked.

Proverbs 23:17

Don't envy evil men but continue to reverence the Lord all the time, for surely you have a wonderful future ahead of you.

Prayer

Dear Lord, preserve the President, who reverences Your name and seeks to do Your will daily in the decision making areas of defense, foreign affairs, energy conservation, and every kind of issue vital to our world. The weight of responsibility is so heavy upon him O Lord. May Your blessed Holy Spirit lead him aright in every issue. In Christ's name I pray.

My Concerns Today

_____

_____

_____

_____

My Concerns Today

_____

_____

_____

_____

July 3

Hosea 10:13

But you have cultivated wickedness and raised a thriving crop of sins. You have earned the full reward of trusting in a lie believing that military might and great armies can make a nation safe.

Prayer

Dear Lord God, forgive our people, that as in other nations we have put our faith in military power. Now, O Lord, bless the President as tries to listen to You and the teachings of Your Holy Word.

July 4

Proverbs 14:34

Godliness exalts a nation, but sin is a reproach to any people.

Prayer

Dear Father God, reveal Yourself and Your love to us and teach us how to live. How we have failed You as a nation – as individuals – only You fully know. On this Day of Independence, as I pray for the President, I pray for all our public officials and for our citizens. Help each of us rededicate ourselves to live godly lives that as a nation we may more perfectly please You, our God. In Christ's name.

My Concerns Today

_____
_____
_____
_____

My Concerns Today

_____
_____
_____
_____

Psalm 105:7

He is the Lord our God. His good-ness is seen everywhere throughout the land.

Prayer

Dear Father, You are the great Source and Provider of all the beauty of land, sea and sky which we behold. We thank You for this beautiful land of ours – this land we call America. We thank You for the birth of this nation and the people You have used to make it great. Now I pray for the President to lead us all into a new stage of growth in the deeper search of Your divine plan for our nation as witness to Your majesty. Let others see in our dealings with all nations those principles which bring honor to You. In Christ's name I pray.

Daniel 2:20-22

He (God) alone has all wisdom and all power. World events are under His control....He gives wise men their wisdom, and scholars their in-telligence. He reveals profound mys-teries beyond man's understanding. He knows all hidden things, for He is light, and darkness is no obstacle to Him.

Prayer

Dear Lord, You honored Daniel with great understanding of things that were absolute mysteries to others. I beseech You to give such knowledge and understanding to the President in dealing with other nations. Reveal to him Your will, O Lord. In Christ's name I pray.

My Concerns Today

_____
_____
_____
_____

My Concerns Today

_____
_____
_____
_____

July 7

Matthew 16:25

And everyone who loses his life for Me shall find it again.

Prayer

Dear Lord, our Savior has taught us that when we give freely, joyously, with full measure, that our giving will be multiplied back to us in full measure. We are believing this for the President as he gives up his privacy, his personal freedom, and all of the benefits of a successful private business life. He accepts responsibilities greater than anyone of us can imagine. Now I pray for Your fulfillment of unlimited blessings in this life which he has laid down in trust for You. In Christ's name I pray.

July 8

Psalm 94:14-15

The Lord will not forsake His people, for they are His prize. Judgment will again be just and all the upright will rejoice.

Prayer

Dear Lord, although we Americans have sinned in many ways, we know You will not forsake us. Through more than 200 years the people of our nation who loved and honored You have given their lives, their fortunes, their talents, and their strength to build a country. We have cherished freedom and morality, law and order, development and education of each individual. Therefore I pray the President will uphold such beliefs and give of himself now to the accomplishment of Your will in these matters.

My Concerns Today

_____

_____

_____

_____

My Concerns Today

_____

_____

_____

_____

July 9

Psalm 94:19

Lord, when doubts fill my mind, when my heart is in turmoil, quiet me and give me renewed hope and cheer.

Prayer

Dear Lord God, send the blessed peace, renewed hope of the Spirit of Your loving Son into the mind and heart of the President this very day. And my prayer is that each time any doubt fills his mind, or turmoil fills his heart that Your blessed peace will flow into him and renew his hope, strengthen his will, and set him on the right course again. Bless his soul, O my Lord, in Christ's name.

My Concerns Today

_____

_____

_____

_____

July 10

Psalm 91:1

We live within the shadow of the Almighty, sheltered by the God Who is above all gods.

.

Prayer

Dear Lord, Almighty and Everlasting God, Who sent Your Holy Spirit to be our constant comfort, our glorious guide, a perpetual presence of Your own Blessed Self, we praise You. You, the God above all gods, are the God who has brought the President to the place where he is this day. You allow him to live in Your shadow. How gracious and how blessed he is. And for all this I pray the prayer of thankfulness for the people of this country. In Christ's name.

My Concerns Today

_____

_____

_____

_____

Psalm 90:16-17

Let us see Your miracles again; let our children see glorious things, the kind You used to do, and let the Lord, our God, favor us and give us success.

Prayer

Dear Lord, we praise You for our President. We believe that You are the miracle working God. We thank You and praise You for every miracle that You perform which blesses our people. Make us a nation that gives You all the praise. You are the God of the Universe and know our every need. We praise You, O God.

Philippians 2:13

For God is at work within you, helping you want to obey Him, and then helping you do what He wants.

Prayer

Dear Lord God, thank You for this promise to Your redeemed children that You are at work in us, helping us to obey and helping us do what Christ wants us to do. We thank You for the saints of old, for the recorders of Your Word, and especially for St. Paul. We claim this promise You made through Paul, that in our President You are at work. You are helping him daily to obey the commandments of our Lord. Through him as a clean vessel we expect You to do a mighty work. For this we thank You today in Christ's name.

My Concerns Today

_____

_____

_____

_____

My Concerns Today

_____

_____

_____

_____

James 5:10-11

For examples of patience in suffering, look at the Lord's prophets. We know how happy they are now because they stayed true to Him then, even though they suffered greatly for it.

Prayer

Dear Lord, no matter how difficult the tasks of the President, or how great the pressure from opposing minds, or how severe the criticisms from people or the press I pray that the Holy Spirit will give him patience. We know that he must endure mental, emotional, and spiritual suffering to persevere in the paths where You lead him. We pray constantly for his strength to endure the suffering and that he will remain true to You.

My Concerns Today

_____
_____
_____
_____

Psalm 91:11

For He orders His angels to protect you wherever you go.

Prayer

Dear Lord God, how we thank You that You have given us the blessings of protection by angels assigned to us. You are so great and mighty, yet You are loving and gracious. Every action and every circumstance of our lives are of importance to You. We have seen and known of circumstances in which the angels You sent to guard and care for us saved us from great danger or disaster. Praise Your name, O Lord, for the President's angels whom You have assigned to his care and protection. In Christ's name.

My Concerns Today

_____
_____
_____
_____

Philippians 1:9-10

My prayer for you is that you will overflow more and more with love for others, and at the same time keep on growing in spiritual knowledge and insight, for I want you always to see clearly the difference between right and wrong.

Prayer

Dear Lord, this is my prayer for the President that as he continues to grow in Your love he will pour forth that love towards people. Yet, at the same time, O Lord, keep him growing in spiritual knowledge and insight. All of us who are Christians must surely want, and pray for him to see clearly the difference between right and wrong in every issue he faces. Help him, dear Lord.

My Concerns Today

_____

_____

_____

_____

Isaiah 42:21-22

The Lord has magnified His law and made it truly glorious. Through it He had planned to show the world that He is righteous. But what sight His people are — these who were to demonstrate to all the world the glory of His law.

Prayer

Dear Father, help the President as he tries in all areas of our life to set our eyes and hearts upon Your law, that the United States may glorify You, before all the world, as the righteous God. Forgive us, O Lord, for all of our failure to honor Christ in our national life. In Christ's name.

My Concerns Today

_____

_____

_____

_____

Isaiah 43:1-2

I have called you by name; you are Mine. When you go through deep waters and great trouble, I will be with you. When you go through rivers of difficulty, you will not drown!

Prayer

Dear Lord God, the President has been through some deep waters during his term so far, but we praise You for keeping Your promise to be with him. Please, Lord, keep the President always under Your divine protection.

Isaiah 45:22-23

Let all the world look to Me for salvation! For I am God; there is no other. I have sworn by Myself and I will never go back on My word, for it is true — that every knee in all the world shall bow to Me, and every tongue shall swear allegiance to My name.

Prayer

Dear Lord, bless the President as he meets and talks with other world leaders. Send Your Holy Spirit to be in their midst. May Your Spirit sharpen their intellects, soothe their emotions, and endow the spirits of all with patience and understanding toward one another. In Your blessed name I pray.

My Concerns Today

_____
_____
_____
_____

My Concerns Today

_____
_____
_____
_____

July 19

Lamentations 3:40-42

Let us examine ourselves instead, and repent, and turn again to the Lord. Let us lift our hearts and hands to Him in heaven, for we have sinned; we have rebelled against the Lord, and He has not forgotten it.

Prayer

Dear Lord God, our nation has sinned in many areas. In education we have forsaken discipline for license, calling it freedom. Now after years of false teachings our young ravage the old and our streets are unsafe. When the lights are out in many cities the undisciplined revert from decency and order to unrestrained looting and destruction. Help the President, O Lord, to call attention of our leaders to the disgrace of crime in our Christian land.

My Concerns Today

_____

_____

_____

_____

July 20

Psalm 44:1

O God, we have heard of the glorious miracles You did in the days of long ago.

Prayer

Dear Lord God, we pray today for the President to remember that Your way must always include good for all Your children. Our hearts cry out for peace, but Your children must have peace in their hearts before the nations can have peace. Bless the President in all deliberations. In Christ's name.

My Concerns Today

_____

_____

_____

_____

Proverbs 25:15

Be patient and you will finally win, for a soft tongue can break hard bones.

Prayer

Dear Lord God, since a soft answer turns away wrath and love is stronger than evil, we see in the President the capacity to be patient, to speak gently and softly, not in weakness but in strength. We thank You for that. Bless the President in his tremendous expressions in mind, body and speech to evidence his patience and self-control in all situations. As he must take part in many conferences, interviews and confrontations, we praise and bless You for giving him wisdom and self-discipline. In Christ's name.

Isaiah 28:12-13

They could have rest in their own land if they would obey Him, if they were kind and good. He told them that but they wouldn't listen to Him. So the Lord will spell it out for them.

Prayer

Dear Lord, the Jewish people have had such a long, hard way to follow. They have sinned but they have been punished. I pray for the President who through the power of the Holy Spirit loves all people, to be able to help Israel find a good life and peace with their neighbors. All of the international relationships are so involved, dear Lord, that I do not even understand the whole problem. I pray You will give the President full understanding through Your Holy Spirit. In Christ's name.

My Concerns Today

_____

_____

_____

_____

My Concerns Today

_____

_____

_____

_____

Matthew 11:28-30

Come to Me and I will give you rest – all of you who work so hard beneath a heavy yoke. Wear My yoke – for it fits perfectly – and let Me teach you; for I am gentle and humble, and you shall find rest for your souls.

Prayer

Dear Lord God, thank You for the President who bears a heavy yoke of leadership for this country. We thank You for his abilities and his past experiences. We pray this day for You, Lord, to give him divine wisdom. May his leadership be ever directed toward service in Your name.

2 Timothy 2:19

But God's truth stands firm like a great rock and nothing can shake it. It is a foundation stone with these words written on it: "The Lord knows those who are really His."

Prayer

Dear God, bless the President with faith in You and in democracy that our founding fathers had. They recognized that because of the differences in men there would be many problems. But they were hopeful that under divine leadership the intelligent use of certain principles would lead to solutions to all national problems. Bless the members of our Congress, O Lord, to Your honor and glory. In Christ's name.

My Concerns Today

_____

_____

_____

_____

My Concerns Today

_____

_____

_____

_____

Mark 1:34

But He replied, "We must go on to other towns as well and give My message to them too, for that is why I came."

Prayer

Dear Father, as we sang, "We've a story to tell to the nations, that shall turn their hearts to the right – a story of truth and mercy – a story of peace and light," (words and tune: Message, H. Ernest Nichol, 1896) I prayed for the President. May he pray daily for the "message" You send to other nations concerning our relationships with them. I pray that he sends out Your message, O Lord, and so I beseech You to help him, his Cabinet and the Congress. Help us send out Your message of righteousness, peace and brotherhood. In Christ's name I pray.

John 3:17

God did not send His Son into the world to condemn it, but to save it.

Prayer

Dear Father God, we ask Your blessing on all Your children everywhere, who name the name of Your Son as their Savior. May the Christian people throughout the United States cooperate with their leaders to bring peace in the world as they unite in spirit with the President. O Lord, give all the wisdom and virtues of a true follower to the President as he confers with heads of state. Lead our nations in righteous cooperation. In Christ's name.

My Concerns Today

_____

_____

_____

_____

My Concerns Today

_____

_____

_____

_____

Galatians 6:9

Let us not get tired of doing what is right, for after a while we will reap a harvest of blessing if we don't get discouraged and give up.

Prayer

Dear Lord, I pray for the President to be supplied with the strength of mind, body and spirit not to give up but to persevere with faith in the solution of the various problems. Even though it may appear that some nations are not cooperating as they should, we pray for them and for the President. Let all who work on these problems be led by Your Spirit to advance Your peace among the nations involved. Let this settlement of problems be a witness to all nations that Your righteousness reigns. In His name I pray.

My Concerns Today

_____

_____

_____

_____

Psalm 84:11

For Jehovah God is our Light and our Protector, He gives us grace and glory. No good thing will be withheld from those who walk along His paths.

Prayer

Dear Lord, I pray for the President to be a faithful and trustful follower of God who is our Light and our Protector. I pray he will be a faithful servant of the people who trust him. I believe You, God, will not withhold from him any good thing he needs to be a good leader as well as a good man. O Lord, we are counting on You to hold up his hands and his heart. In Christ's name.

My Concerns Today

_____

_____

_____

_____

2 Timothy 2:13

Even when we are too weak to have any faith left, He remains faithful to us and will help us, for He cannot disown us who are part of Himself, and He will always carry out His promise to us.

Prayer

Dear Lord, if the President has weak moments or periods of weariness, please sustain, strengthen and refresh him. You have given us Your promise to always be with us. No doubt, the many complexities which the President deals with demand great physical effort and mental anguish at times. We are trusting Your faithfulness to sustain him. In Christ's name I pray.

My Concerns Today

_____

_____

_____

_____

1 Peter 2:6

As the Scriptures express it, "See, I am sending Christ to be the carefully chosen, precious Cornerstone of My church, and I will never disappoint those who trust in Him."

Prayer

Dear Father, we know You are blessing the President. You have promised You will never disappoint those who trust in Jesus Christ, Your Son. May the President remain true to every moral and spiritual truth learned from the Christ. Help him, O Lord, to deal with all of life on the grounds of those truths. In Christ's name.

My Concerns Today

_____

_____

_____

_____

1 Peter 2:15

It is God's will that your good lives should silence those who foolishly condemn the Gospel without knowing what it can do for them, having never experienced its power.

Prayer

O Lord, I pray that during this administration, we shall see evidences of moral and spiritual renewal among the people that they may experience the power of the Gospel in their own lives through the influence of the President's life. In Christ's name I pray.

My Concerns Today

_____

_____

_____

_____

Psalm 96:7-8

O nations of the world, confess that God alone is glorious and strong. Give Him the glory He deserves! Bring Him your offering and come to worship Him.

Prayer

Dear Lord God, bless the President and our national leaders as they represent not only our country to the other nations, but You as our God. We know You are the God of all nations. We also are aware that many nations do not honor You as our nation was founded to do. Oh, dear Lord, make our nation strong and honorable in all its dealings with other nations for Your name's sake.

My Concerns Today

_____

_____

_____

_____

Proverbs 3:4-6

If you want favor with both God and man, and a reputation for good judgment and common sense, then trust the Lord completely; don't ever trust yourself. In everything you do, put God first and He will direct you and crown your efforts with success.

Prayer

Dear Lord God, we pray that the President has studied Your Word and knows from that study as well as from experience that he can trust You completely. This is not easy. We often say and think these words and then fail to live by them. We pray for him this day to have the power to completely trust You.

My Concerns Today

_____

_____

_____

_____

August 3

Deuteronomy 4:6

If you obey them (the laws of God), they will give you a reputation for wisdom and intelligence.

Prayer

Dear Lord God, as I pray for the President, I praise You and ask You to bless him with wisdom in each governmental decision he makes. As he faces each responsibility, may the words most needed from Your Holy Word come to his mind. If he opens the Bible to read of You, O God, may Your message leap from the page to guide him in his earnest quest to do Your will. In Christ's name.

August 4

Exodus 20:13

You must not murder.

Genesis 9:5-6

Murder is forbidden...for to kill a man is to kill one made like God.

Prayer

Dear Lord God, I beseech You to sustain and strengthen the President and others of our government who are opposed to killing the innocent. It is wrong for our government to condone this. We are guilty of murdering those You created in Your image. We know man is the instrument used by You to produce new life but that You are the Creator of all life. Oh, God, forgive our sins and save our people. In Christ's name.

My Concerns Today

_____

_____

_____

_____

My Concerns Today

_____

_____

_____

_____

Ezekiel 13:22-23

Your lies have discouraged the righteous, when I didn't want it so. And you have encouraged the wicked by promising life, though they continue in their sins…I will deliver My people out of your hands by destroying you, and you shall know I am the Lord.

Prayer

Dear Lord God, I pray that the President will be made aware of the breaking of Your laws in the national movement afoot to give life through freedom and equal rights to the homosexual agenda. This agenda defies Your law and causes people to live in sin. Let the President realize the extent of the spread of immorality if, through legislation, we sanction and promote such irreverence for You, the Almighty God.

My Concerns Today

_____

_____

_____

_____

Philemon 6

I pray that as you share your faith with others, it will grip their lives too, as they see the wealth of good things in you that come from Christ Jesus.

Prayer

Dear Lord God, I pray today for the President, for all his Cabinet and members of the Congress. As he shares with them his ideas of integrity, may they all be strengthened. Dear Lord, give them an extra endowment of Your love and grace. May all that is done by them be for Your glory and honor. In Christ's name.

My Concerns Today

_____

_____

_____

_____

Psalm 119:124-125

Lord, deal with me in loving kindness, and teach me, your servant, to obey; for I am your servant; therefore give me common sense to apply Your rules to everything I do.

Prayer

Dear Lord God, I pray You this day to bring to the President's mind Your truths which will strengthen him. At the same time may my petition be joined with his as he asks You, the Source of all wisdom, to give him common sense. I humbly beseech You to answer this prayer in my behalf, also, that I, Your servant, may apply common sense in all that I do. In Christ's name I pray.

Matthew 20:26-28

Anyone wanting to be a leader among you must be your servant. And if you want to be right at the top, you must serve like a slave. Your attitude must be like my own, for I, the Messiah, did not come to be served, but to serve, and to give My life as a ransom for many.

Prayer

Dear Lord God, bless our President in his service to the people of this nation and to the world as he attempts to practice Your teachings. We realize that our service to others, if lifted up and dedicated as a service to You, can bless others in a very special way. In Christ's name.

My Concerns Today

_____
_____
_____
_____

My Concerns Today

_____
_____
_____
_____

Mark 8:33

You are looking at this only from a human point of view, and not from God's.

Prayer

Dear Lord, we recall that Jesus rebuked even His apostle Peter when Peter failed to understand that Christ's approaching death was a part of God's plan. From a human's point of view it seemed incredibly wrong. We now understand, Lord, You had to suffer if You obeyed Your Father. So, the President may have to look at many problems from Your point of view, and not from the human point of view. Help him, Lord, to look from Your point of view for solutions which are just and of eternal value. In Christ's name.

My Concerns Today

_____

_____

_____

_____

Romans 12:2

Don't copy the behavior and customs of this world, but be a new and different person with a fresh newness in all you do and think.

Prayer

Dear Father God, the President is a new and different President from every other one we've ever had. We thank You for the newness and the different talents and abilities of this President and of each member of his Cabinet. And we pray that each one will rededicate himself and his various abilities to cope with the responsibilities of government which each one has. Renew freshness and newness each day, O Lord, as a fresh and flowing spring whose waters have no end. In Christ's name.

My Concerns Today

_____

_____

_____

_____

Romans 12:3

As God's messenger I give each of you God's warning. Be honest in your estimate of yourselves, measuring your value by how much faith God has given you.

Prayer

Dear Lord, teach our President through Your Holy Spirit to be honest in his estimate of himself, measuring his value by how much faith You have given him. You alone, O Lord God, know the extent of Your belief in and plans for greatness in this President of ours. Our nation, and our world are crying out to You in longing for true greatness in a leader. I do believe You have chosen him as Your ambassador among the national leaders at this time. Thank You, Father.

My Concerns Today

_____
_____
_____
_____

Hebrews 11:33-34

These people all trusted God and as a result won battles, overthrew kingdoms, ruled their people well, and received what God had promised them; they were kept from harm in a den of lions, and in a fiery furnace. Some through their faith, escaped death by the sword. Some were made strong again after they had been weak or sick. Others were given great power in battle; they make whole armies turn and run away.

Prayer

Dear Lord, we do not know the special and personal promises You have made to our President as he made his commitment to You, but we praise You and trust You that he may keep those promises. And we thank You for them. In Christ's name.

My Concerns Today

_____
_____
_____
_____

James 1:5

If you want to know what God wants you to do, ask Him, and He will gladly tell you, for He is always ready to give a bountiful supply of wisdom to all who ask Him.

Prayer

Dear Lord, please give to the President the bountiful supply of wisdom You have promised to those who know You, trust You, and serve You. May he know he is doing this. May he trust You for wisdom and guidance. May he make wise decisions of State. May he be led to make wise decisions as he deals with representatives of other nations. May he rear and guide his own children in the nurture of the Lord. Bless him, O Lord.

James 2:22

You see, he was trusting God so much that he was willing to do whatever God told him to; his faith was made complete by what he did, by his actions, his good deeds.

Prayer

Dear Lord, Our President faces the questions and criticisms of his time in office. Let him feel Your Presence strongly supporting him. We pray that he has obeyed You. He has done what he could about many problems; some critics say he hasn't done enough, while others say he has tried to do too much. But You alone know the full extent of this obedience to Your guiding hand. In Christ's name I pray for him.

My Concerns Today

_____

_____

_____

_____

My Concerns Today

_____

_____

_____

_____

James 4:6-8

As the Scripture says, God gives strength to the humble, but sets Himself against the proud and haughty. So give yourselves humbly to God. Resist the devil and he will flee from you. And when you draw close to God, God will draw close to you.

Prayer

Dear Lord, I beseech You to send a very special blessing upon our President and his wife at this time. We know their faith will be giving them strength. As they draw close to You during this time of special problems, we know You will draw close to them. Every day he serves as our President may he find the strength he needs through Your divine protection. In Christ's name I pray.

Psalm 46:1-2,10

God is our refuge and strength, a tested help in times of trouble. And so we need not fear even if the world blows up, and the mountains crumble to the sea. "Stand silent! Know that I am God! I will be honored by every nation in the world."

Prayer

Dear Lord God, thank You for our President. May he be honored by every nation on earth. We ask You to bless him. Let him know that modern living and rigorous responsibilities tend to invade the quiet sanctuary of his soul. Protect him from this erosion and keep his soul in peace. I pray in Christ's name.

My Concerns Today

_____
_____
_____
_____

My Concerns Today

_____
_____
_____
_____

Mark 4:11

You are permitted to know some truths about the Kingdom of God that are hidden to those outside the Kingdom.

Prayer

Dear Lord God, You have blessed this man for whom I pray at this moment, the President of our great country. You have chosen to endow him with physical strength and brilliant mind. You have blessed him with a charming personality and an empathetic spirit. I beseech You, therefore, to continue Your endowment of him with revealed truths which only those of Your Kingdom are permitted to possess, that his leadership in world affairs may glorify Your name.

My Concerns Today

_____

_____

_____

_____

Ephesians 5:28

That is how husbands should treat their wives, loving them as parts of themselves. For since a man and his wife are now one, a man is really doing himself a favor and loving himself when he loves his wife.

Proverbs 12:4

A worthy wife is her husband's joy and crown.

Prayer

Dear Lord God, thank You for our President and his wife and their beautiful love for one another. Keep them virtuous, pure, and faithful to You. May the love of our President and his wife for one another be as a rare plant which produces blossoms more beautiful and bountiful with the passing of the seasons. Bless their example of marital fidelity to Your glory, O Lord.

My Concerns Today

_____

_____

_____

_____

Romans 14:13

So don't criticize each other any more. Try instead to live in such a way that you will never make your brother stumble by letting him see you doing something he thinks is wrong.

Prayer

Dear Lord, we pray that our President has set a very high standard of behavior for himself and every member of his staff and every member of Congress. Therefore we pray for them earnestly to turn to You every day for the wisdom and guidance they need to solve every problem of government. Only from Your divine counsel can they honor You as You deserve to be honored. In Christ's name.

My Concerns Today

---

1 Samuel 12:24

Trust the Lord and sincerely worship Him; think of all the tremendous things He has done for you.

Prayer

Dear Lord, thank You for the tremendous things You have done in our President's life. You alone know the full extent of Your plan for this life. Your love created him. Your wisdom guided him through the work of Your Spirit. Your Son died for him. Your angels have traveled from heaven to earth on countless missions to protect him. Your Holy Word teaches and guides him. Your people give him fellowship. We worship You and praise You, Almighty and loving Father, for this one of Your children. In our Savior's name, we thank You.

My Concerns Today

Psalm 103: 1-5, 13

I bless the holy name of God with all my heart. Yes, I will bless the Lord and not forget the glorious things He does for me. He forgives all my sins. He heals me. He ransoms me from hell. He surrounds me with loving kindness and tender mercies. He fills my life with good things….He is like a father to us, tender and sympathetic to those who reverence Him.

Prayer

Dear Lord, as I read this Psalm over and over today, I give You the glory, the praise and the adoration as expressed by the Psalmist. Out of my love for You and my respect and good will for the President, I pray for You to bless, forgive and heal him. May You surround him with lovingkindness and tender mercies. In Christ's name.

My Concerns Today

_____
_____
_____
_____

Proverbs 28:26

A man is a fool to trust himself! But those who use God's wisdom are safe.

Proverbs 29:18

Where there is ignorance of God, the people run wild; but what a wonderful thing it is for a nation to know and keep His laws!

Prayer

Dear Lord God, our President is not a fool. He does not trust himself. He trusts You, Almighty God. Our nation, on the other hand, has some people in it who are running wild and hurting others and themselves and dishonoring Your holy name. When our leaders dishonored You in the public schools, we set in progress a decline in obedience and respect for You and Your laws of righteousness. Place this condition upon our President's heart I pray.

My Concerns Today

_____
_____
_____
_____

Lamentations 3:55-57

But I called upon Your name, O Lord, from deep within the well, and You heard me! You listened to my pleading; You heard my weeping! Yes, You came at my despairing cry and told me not to fear.

Prayer

Dear Lord, at times I can imagine that our President must feel that he is indeed in a deep well with water over his head, and no way left him by which he can change any of his circumstances. It may be that even through the act of son, friend, or coworker, he feels overwhelmed. But You can speak to his heart at any time and go to him with comforting words. I pray, Lord, that You will listen to his pleading and hear his cries for help. For all this I praise and thank you, Lord.

My Concerns Today

_____

_____

_____

_____

Zechariah 10:12

The Lord says, "I will make My people strong with power from Me! They will go wherever they wish, and wherever they go, they will be under My personal care."

Prayer

Dear Lord God, I believe that all of us who have accepted Jesus Christ as our Savior are now Your children. I believe that You give to each of us strength wherever we go and whatever we do. So as I pray for our President this day. Give him not only strength but the sense of Your Holy Spirit's presence and guidance. In Christ's name.

My Concerns Today

_____

_____

_____

_____

Psalm 56:9-12

This very day I call for help, the tide of battle turns. My enemies flee! This one thing I know! God is for me! I am trusting God – oh, praise His promises! I am not afraid of anything mere man can do to me! Yes, praise His promises. I will surely do what I have promised, Lord, and thank You for Your help.

Prayer

Dear Lord, keep our President unafraid of any of the conniving tricks of his adversaries – with trust so grounded in You that the song of confidence still rings in his heart and on his lips. He has many faithful friends. May his friends who counsel him be led to speak only Your will. In Christ's name I pray.

Psalm 89:5-8

All heaven shall praise Your miracles, O Lord; myriads of angels will praise You for Your faithfulness. For who in all of heaven can be compared with God? What mightiest angel is anything like Him? The highest of angelic powers stand in dread and awe of Him. Who is as revered as He by those surrounding Him? O Jehovah, Commander of the heavenly armies, where is there any other Mighty One like You? Faithfulness is Your very character.

Prayer

Dear Lord God, with complete trust in Your faithfulness, we pray for our President, that he may be the recipient this day of Your gracious and loving concern. In Christ's name.

My Concerns Today

_____

_____

_____

_____

My Concerns Today

_____

_____

_____

_____

Romans 8:25

But if we must keep trusting God for something that hasn't happened yet, it teaches us to wait patiently and confidently.

Prayer

Dear Lord, the President has possibly worked for, hoped for, and expected certain accomplishments which have not been realized at this time. I pray for You to bless him with renewed faith, teaching him to wait patiently and confidently until such achievements are realized. Let his heart sing the song of David "I wait patiently for the Lord." With love and faith I pray for him, in the name of Christ.

My Concerns Today

_____

_____

_____

_____

1 Kings 8:57-58

May the Lord our God be with us as He was with our fathers; may He never forsake us. May He give us the desire to do His will in everything, and to obey all the commandments and instructions He has given our ancestors.

Prayer

Dear Lord God, give the President an open mind ready to receive new knowledge. Give him courage to change his mind when that is needed. Give him open ears to hear the human cries of all kinds that ascend from the lowliest huts to The White House. Give him open eyes to see You in the high and mighty, as well as in the poor and lowly. Give him open hands and heart as he shares the bounties that You have given him with those You bring into his orbit. In Christ's name.

My Concerns Today

_____

_____

_____

_____

John 8:12

Later in one of His talks, Jesus said to the people, "I am the light of the world. So if you follow Me, you won't be stumbling through the darkness, for living light will flood your path."

Prayer

Dear Lord God, let the President see more clearly every day. As he walks through tunnels of darkness, by looking to Jesus Christ each day he will see the truest light. Give him grace to understand that the world he cannot see or touch is the most real world of all. Help him to keep steadily in his mind that the things that matter are not money, possessions, land, power, or bodily comfort but truth, honor, meekness, service to others and love of Christ.

My Concerns Today

_____

_____

_____

_____

Ephesians 1:11

For as part of God's sovereign plan, we were chosen from the beginning to be His, and all things happen just as He decided long ago.

Prayer

Dear Lord God, as I pray this morning for the President, I believe in and acknowledge Your Sovereign plan for his life. Allow me, O Lord, to humbly pray these blessings for him this day. Let him be a Christian in word and deed this day. Let him be hard and stern with himself. Let his thinking be clear and keen, his speech be frank and open, and his actions courageous and decisive. Let him this day so reflect the spirit of Christ in every way that You may be glorified.

My Concerns Today

_____

_____

_____

_____

Deuteronomy 29:29

There are secrets the Lord your God has not revealed to us, but these words He has revealed are for us and our children to obey forever.

Prayer

Dear Lord God, thank You for these secrets You have revealed to us through Your Holy Word. Bless the President as he leans heavily upon these secrets and promises. You are the one and only God, all powerful, but loving and merciful. You demand obedience and provide a Source of wisdom – Your Holy Word. You have provided a Savior for us and have promised Your presence to all who believe and trust You. In Christ's name I thank You.

My Concerns Today

_____

_____

_____

_____

September 1

Titus 2:1

But as for you, speak for the right living that goes along with true Christianity.

Prayer

Dear Lord God, how we thank You for the President. May our people pray daily for him. We need to pray that he will seek Your divine guidance. His responsibilities as our leader are different from ours. However, Lord, we ask You to teach us constantly our responsibility as citizens. In Christ's name.

September 2

Titus 3:2

Be gentle and truly courteous to all.

Prayer

Dear Lord God, we pray that the President of our country will always act as a gentleman. We pray that no matter how provoking or critical or argumentative anyone is toward him, he may respond to such behavior with love, gentleness, patience and courtesy. Our Savior, Who taught us to turn the other cheek and to bless those who persecute us, must be very pleased when He sees followers of His so faithfully reflecting His spirit of love no matter who trying the circumstances. Bless the President, O Lord, and sustain him in every circumstance. In Christ's name I pray.

My Concerns Today

_____
_____
_____
_____

My Concerns Today

_____
_____
_____
_____

Psalm 1:2

But they (those who love God) delight in doing everything God wants them to, and day and night are always meditating on His laws and thinking about ways to follow Him more closely.

Prayer

Dear Lord, we pray that the President may have a pattern of early morning meditation. During that time he can draw close to You – meditate on You, Your righteousness, Your love – and think of ways in which he can follow You more closely. Bless him, O Lord, and direct his thoughts and his deeds as a "peacemaker" in the affairs of our nation. In Christ's name.

My Concerns Today

_____

_____

_____

_____

Proverbs 2:6,9

For the Lord grants wisdom; His every word is a treasure of knowledge and understanding. He shows how to distinguish right from wrong, how to find the right decision every time.

Prayer

Dear Lord God, no doubt the President seeks Your guidance. No doubt he prays for wisdom. No doubt he studies and thinks, confers and deliberates. No doubt he wants to know right from wrong regarding every issue upon which he must make a decision. But, dear Lord, even in Your earthly life there were forces of evil exerted against You. May Your Spirit guide him in dealing with those around him who would overly persuade him against Your right decisions. In Christ's name.

My Concerns Today

_____

_____

_____

_____

September 5

Matthew 25:21

His master praised him for good work. "You have been faithful in handling this small amount," he told him, "so now I will give you many more responsibilities. Begin the joyous tasks I have assigned to you."

Prayer

Dear Lord, no man has true respect for himself who does not work for his living. Charity toward those who have no work would be to provide work for them. Please, Lord, reveal some plan to our President and his coworkers by which our unemployed can be given honorable work to do. They need to work, to earn, to be respected and appreciated by others in order to have self-respect. Help our President find a way, O Lord. In Christ's name.

My Concerns Today

_____
_____
_____
_____

September 6

Isaiah 43:11-13

I am the Lord and there is no other Savior. Whenever you have thrown away your idols, I have shown you My power. With one word I have saved you. You have seen Me do it; you are My witnesses that it is true. From eternity to eternity I am God. No one can oppose what I do.

Prayer

Dear Lord, help our President to destroy every idol of complacency, blindness to suffering, self-deception, pride of position, unwillingness to change. Then refill him and renew in him diligence, sincerity, charity for all, long-suffering, courtesy and patience. Enlighten his heart with Your Presence. Reflect Your love through his words and deeds. Keep his joy in Your fellowship glowing. In Christ's name I pray.

My Concerns Today

_____
_____
_____
_____

September 7

Proverbs 11:24

It is possible to give away and become richer! It is also possible to hold on too tightly and lose everything.

Prayer

Dear Lord, You know what is right for us as a nation to do about every problem. As our President seeks Your guidance I pray You to bless him and make him successful only if he is really following Your leadership. O Lord, guide the thinking of our leaders who have the responsibility of understanding every problem and need of the people. I ask only that Your Holy Spirit will pray through me for I know not how to pray. In Christ's name I pray.

September 8

Matthew 6:22-23

If your eye is pure, there will be sunshine in your soul. But if your eye is clouded with evil thoughts and desires, you are in deep spiritual darkness. And oh, how deep that darkness can be!

Prayer

Dear Lord, we pray that the face of our President will show the confidence of one who looks at life with a pure eye and has sunshine in his soul. We thank You for this reflection of Your peace in his soul. We ask that his poise, quietness of manner, and gentleness with all people will spread through our nation. May we be individuals who treat others as we wish to be treated. In Christ's name I pray.

My Concerns Today

_____
_____
_____
_____

My Concerns Today

_____
_____
_____
_____

Matthew 7:24

All who listen to My instructions and follow them are wise, like a man who builds his house on solid rock.

Prayer

Dear Lord, teach our President and his Cabinet to listen not only to one another, but to You. May each one train himself to listen also to You and to Your Holy Spirit as He speaks to each of them. May the instructions You have given in Your Word become the rock of wisdom and truth to each one. Thus will our nation be built upon the solid rock of truth and righteousness. In Christ's name.

Philippians 2:5-6

Your attitude should be the kind that was shown us by Jesus Christ, who, though He was God, did not demand and cling to His rights as God.

Prayer

Dear Lord, help the President always to keep in the front of his mind as he faces each problem "What would Jesus do?" and then do it. O Lord, the President needs your constant and perfect guidance as he brings to the Oval Office this idea of what Jesus would do. Can a nation's leader act *for a nation* on the same premise? As a nation, can we use and should we think of the welfare of other nations above the welfare of our own? Bless our President in Jesus' name.

My Concerns Today

_____
_____
_____
_____

My Concerns Today

_____
_____
_____
_____

Joshua 1:17-18

May the Lord your God be with you as He was with Moses…so lead on with courage and strength!

Prayer

Dear Lord, our people know our President to be a man who is just and true, who believes in honor and integrity, who acts towards others with courtesy and generosity, and who is loyal to friends and magnanimous toward opponents. But I now pray, dear Lord, that our President will never rest content until he has given his all to You – that total commitment which will seek the fullness of the graces, faith, hope, and love and bring him into a perfect walk with Christ. In His name I pray.

My Concerns Today

_____

_____

_____

_____

1 Corinthians 3:20-21

In the book of Psalms, we are told that the Lord knows full well how the human mind reasons, and how foolish and futile it is. So don't be proud of following the wise man of this world. For God has already given you everything you need.

Prayer

Dear Lord, today we pray for our President and place him respectfully under Your divine guidance. From You let him seek guidance in the filling of any office that needs to be filled. Raise up, O Lord, the person You have chosen for that place of great responsibility. Then make our President aware of him. In Christ's name.

My Concerns Today

_____

_____

_____

_____

September 13

Matthew 17:20

If you had faith even as small as a tiny mustard seed, you could say to this mountain, "Move!" and it would go far away. Nothing would be impossible.

Prayer

Dear Lord God, in praise and adoration I pray to You, our Father and our God, that day by day as our President lives by faith he shall see You move mountains. Keep his faith intact as he works for peace on international problems. You have showered our President with richness of Your grace, O Lord. You are using him for Your own holy presence. Nothing is impossible with You. In Christ's name.

September 14

Matthew 18:15,21-22

If a brother sins against you, go to him privately and confront him with his fault. If he listens and confesses it, you have won back a brother....Then Peter came to him and asked, "Sir, how often should I forgive a brother who sins against me? Seven times?" "No," Jesus replied, "Seventy times seven!"

Prayer

Dear Lord, as I pray for our President today, I ask You to give him the spirit of humility. If there is need for him to forgive anyone today or any day, may he remember this admonishment. We are all to remember that there is no limit to the number of times we are to forgive. In Christ's name.

My Concerns Today

_____

_____

_____

_____

My Concerns Today

_____

_____

_____

_____

September 15

Acts 17:27-28

His purpose in all of this is that they should seek after God…For in Him we live and move and are…We are the sons of God.

Prayer

Dear Lord, may our President seek to live as a true son of God, honoring Christ by his life. Teach him to use all circumstances to bring forth fruits of holiness in his life – using his disappointments to produce patience – using his successes to give thanks to You – using danger to increase his humility – using the disappointments in friends to increase his own faithfulness to others – using his pain to learn endurance – using his knowledge of Your Word to enhance his fellowship with Christ. In Christ's name I pray for our President.

September 16

Proverbs 17:17

A true friend is always loyal, and a brother is born to help in time of need.

Prayer

Dear Lord, I lift up my soul to You. Bless Your Holy Name. Bless our President for being a man we can respect because of his loyalty to friends and family. As he faces the tasks, decisions and responsibilities of this day, let him feel Your Holy Presence. Let Your truth inform his mind. Let Your graciousness and righteousness rule in his will. Bless him as he works for purer and fairer laws, for peace between the nations, for energy conservation, and for jobs for the unemployed. In Christ's name I pray.

My Concerns Today

_____
_____
_____
_____

My Concerns Today

_____
_____
_____
_____

Hebrews 10:36

You need to keep on patiently doing God's will if you want Him to do for you all that He has promised.

Prayer

Dear Lord, we who believe in You, the Holy and Almighty God, know that we must ever seek to know Your will and then to do Your will. Through the many avenues of communication at Your command, we pray You will convey Your will to our President concerning each major issue before him. Give us guidance to do what is just and right at all times. In Christ's name I pray.

1 John 3:18-19

Let us stop just saying we love people; let us really love them, and show it by our actions. Then we will know for sure by our actions, that we are on God's side…

Prayer

Dear Lord God, as I pray this day for the President I pray also for each member of his Cabinet and each member of our Congress. May all these men make earnest and honest decisions concerning the welfare of our citizens – the poor, the unemployed. Let their actions be guided by Your Spirit of truth, justice, and love. In Christ's name I pray.

My Concerns Today

_____
_____
_____
_____

My Concerns Today

_____
_____
_____
_____

September 19

1 Corinthians 6:19-20

Your own body does not belong to you. For God has bought you with a great price. So use every part of your body to give glory back to God, because He owns it.

Prayer

Dear Lord God, be with our President this day. Keep the edges of his mind keen. Keep his thinking straight and true. Keep his will actively related to Your divine will. Keep his body fit and healthy. Bless him in his dealings with the ministers of State from other countries. May relationships toward peace be established. Believing Christ wants the nations to be at peace, I pray in His Name.

September 20

Acts 9:31

The believers learned how to walk in fear of the Lord and in the comfort of the Holy Spirit.

Prayer

Dear Lord, we who are Your children because of salvation, through Jesus Christ have learned how to walk in fear of You, the Holy God. At the same time we walk in fear, we also walk in comfort, trust and peace through the Presence of Your Holy Spirit. Therefore, now I pray for our President that he may continuously walk in the fear of the Lord and in the comfort of the Holy Spirit. In Christ's blessed Name.

My Concerns Today

_____

_____

_____

_____

My Concerns Today

_____

_____

_____

_____

Matthew 5:6-7

Happy are those who long to be just and good, for they shall be completely satisfied. Happy are the kind and merciful, for they shall be shown mercy.

Prayer

Dear Lord, I pray for an overwhelming sense of Your Presence to bless the mind and heart of our President. May he be kind and merciful in all situations. Day by day give our President true wisdom which comes to us from Your throne of grace. You are always the source of wisdom, truth and comfort. In Christ's name.

My Concerns Today

_____

_____

_____

_____

Proverbs 20:27-28

A man's conscience is the Lord's searchlight, exposing his hidden motives. If a king is kind, honest and fair, his kingdom stands secure.

Prayer

Dear Lord, with great humility and deep gratitude, we thank You for the gift of conscience – for our own, for that of each man and for that conscience within the President. We thank you for the stability of our government. We pray for Your blessings on our leaders and their families. We praise You, our Lord, for teaching us love and loyalty. In Christ's name I pray.

My Concerns Today

_____

_____

_____

_____

Proverbs 25:27-28

Just as it is harmful to eat too much honey, so also it is bad for men to think about all the honors they deserve. A man without self-control is as defenseless as a city with broken down walls.

Prayer

Dear Lord, we thank You for the peace, humility and complete self-control always seen and felt as we watch our President at work. In 50 years, I have seen great self-control exhibited by our presidents and other national leaders. I commend all our leaders to Your constant care and protection. I pray for our nation to exist as a constant example of Your faithfulness. In Jesus Christ's name I pray.

Proverbs 19:23

Reverence for God gives life, happiness, and protection from harm.

Proverbs 18:10

The Lord is a strong fortress. The godly run to Him and we are safe.

Prayer

Dear Lord God, we can understand the deep fellowship of our President and our Vice President because they bear joint burdens of responsibility. We pray your divine blessing on each of them. We honor them because they were chosen by You and the people of this nation as our leaders. We know that You are their strength in every thing. In the name of Christ, their Savior and mine, I pray.

My Concerns Today

_____
_____
_____
_____

My Concerns Today

_____
_____
_____
_____

1 Corinthians 5:8

So let us feast upon Him (Christ) and grow strong in the Christian life, leaving behind us the cancerous old life with all its hatreds and wickedness. Let us feast instead upon the pure bread of honor and sincerity and truth.

Prayer

Dear Lord and Savior of us all, we praise Your name that You have brought us out of many difficult national situations and times of failure to honor You and Your Holy Word. I pray on this day that as the President calls upon You that You will nourish his soul as he feasts upon the bread of the Spirit. In honor, sincerity, and truth, may he lead our nation in the pursuit of Thy Holy will for us as a godly nation. In Christ's name I pray.

My Concerns Today

_____
_____
_____
_____

2 Corinthians 1:5

You can be sure that the more we undergo sufferings for Christ, the more He will shower us with His comfort and encouragement.

Prayer

Dear Father, in the name of Your Blessed Son, I pray Your Spirit will refresh the mind of our President this day. I thank You for the gift of memory You have given to every person. May our President this day recall sacrificial services of other Presidents. By such memories, Lord, remind him of Your faithfulness. In Christ's name I pray.

My Concerns Today

_____
_____
_____
_____

Romans 15:30

Will you be my prayer partners? For the Lord Jesus Christ's sake, and because of your love for me – given to you by the Holy Spirit – pray much with me for my work.

Prayer

Dear Lord, may we pray as God has directed us. By the power of Your Holy Spirit, O Lord, awaken the people of our nation to the powerful support of prayer for our leaders. Turn our minds and hearts back to You that we may be guided in the momentous problems now facing our nation. In the name of Christ I pray.

2 Corinthians 12:10

Since I know it is all for Christ's good, I am quite happy about "the thorn," and about insults and hardships, persecutions and difficulties; for when I am weak, then I am strong – the less I have, the more I depend on Him.

Prayer

Dear Lord, for Christ's glory I pray for our President. He has to deal with leaders of other nations who have different ideas. Most of those people are sincere. Only You, our Holy God, knows who is right and who is not. But I pray especially this day for our President to have divine wisdom in dealing with all such leaders. May Your Spirit, dear Lord, control each one as they confer together. In Christ's name.

My Concerns Today

_____

_____

_____

_____

My Concerns Today

_____

_____

_____

_____

Psalm 147:11-12

But His joy is in those who reverence Him, those who expect Him to be loving and kind. Praise Him, O Jerusalem! Praise your God, O Zion!

Prayer

Dear Lord God, we thank You for Yourself. We thank You for Christ, our Savior, as we read Your Holy Word and pray for our President. We praise and honor You as God of all the nations. You created these nations whose representatives now counsel with the President. Your wisdom and Your plans are so far above our understanding, we simply pray for Your Holy Spirit to be present in each leader, that Your Divine Will may be accomplished for the ultimate good of all nations. In Christ's name I pray.

My Concerns Today

_____
_____
_____
_____

Ephesians 2:16-18

As parts of the same body, our anger against each other has disappeared, for both of us have been reconciled to God. And so the feud ended at last at the cross. And He has brought this Good News of peace to you Gentiles who were very far away from Him, and to us Jews who were near. Now all of us, whether Jews or Gentiles, may come to God the Father with the Holy Spirit's help, because of what Christ has done for us.

Prayer

Dear Lord God, Father of all people, Gentiles and Jews, bless our President as Your instrument for the Holy Spirit to use in bringing together the leaders of many nations. Christ died that all people may be fused into a oneness with Him. I pray in Christ's name.

My Concerns Today

_____
_____
_____
_____

October 1

Matthew 28:18

He (Jesus) told His disciples: "I have been given all authority in heaven and earth."

Prayer

Dear Lord, You are our God, our Creator, our Redeemer. With praise and adoration, we worship You. But so often we fail to believe that all authority is Yours. Our President has been given great authority as the head of our government. But You, O Lord, have the final authority over all people and all the earth. This I pray, in Christ's name.

October 2

1 Peter 4:14

Be happy if you are cursed and insulted for being a Christian, for when that happens the Spirit of God will come upon you with great glory.

Prayer

Dear Lord, in this busy, complex, sin-filled and problem-burdened world, it is not easy to follow in Christ's steps. "Blessed are ye when men shall revile you, and persecute you, and say all manner of evil against you falsely for My sake. Rejoice and be exceeding glad, for great is your reward in heaven." In Christ's name I pray.

My Concerns Today

_____
_____
_____
_____

My Concerns Today

_____
_____
_____
_____

October 3

1 Peter 5:6-7

If you will humble yourselves under the mighty hand of God, in His good time He will lift you up. Let Him have all your worries and cares, for He is always thinking about you and watching everything that concerns you.

Prayer

Dear Lord, I pray that our President will daily find a peace that floods his soul, a joy that fills his heart, a light that illumines his mind. May he learn to cast all his worries and cares upon You that his spirit may be lifted up and his mind freed. In Your will may he find peace; in Your love rest; in Your service joy. In Christ's name I pray.

My Concerns Today

_____
_____
_____
_____

October 4

1 John 5:15

And if we really know He is listening when we talk to Him and make our requests, then we can be sure that He will answer us.

Prayer

Dear Lord God, You have assured us that You hear us, and listen to us when we come into Your Presence with humility and in a state of repentance of our sins. But also You have blessed us with an Advocate who unceasingly intercedes for us – our Lord and Savior, Jesus Christ. You have promised to answer in accordance with Your will for our good. Therefore I pray for our President's highest good as he performs the tasks of his office and as he seeks the best for our nation. In Christ's name I pray.

My Concerns Today

_____
_____
_____
_____

Psalm 33:10-11

With a breath He can scatter the plans of all nations who oppose Him, but His own plan stands forever. His intentions are the same for every generation.

Prayer

Dear Lord, You have revealed Yourself, Your power, and also Your willingness to forgive, through Your Holy Word. In the writings of the Hebrew people they show us that You are a God of power with a divine plan. Individuals and nations may oppose. They will suffer. But Your divine intentional plan for each person and each nation still endures. I pray for our President to receive from Your holy mind the intention You have for every international problem. In Christ's name I pray.

My Concerns Today

_____
_____
_____
_____

Psalm 35:10

From the bottom of my heart praise rises to Him. Where is His equal in all of heaven and earth? Who else protects the weak and helpless from the strong, and the poor and needy from those who would rob them?

Prayer

Dear Lord, there are so many poor and needy in the world today that our hearts ache with sorrow over their destitution. Help our President to find ways to meet the urgent needs of so many. Many need work, not only to meet physical needs, but for self-respect. In a huge country such as ours, are there not means for constructive, purposeful work for these people? Give new ideas, O Lord, to our leaders and the President that this condition may be changed. In Christ's name I pray.

My Concerns Today

_____
_____
_____
_____

Psalm 119:65-66

Lord, I am overflowing with Your blessings, just as You promised. Now teach me good judgment as well as knowledge. For Your laws are my guide.

Prayer

Dear Lord, we thank You for Your many blessings with which You have crowned our President's past life and work. Now, O Lord, teach him good judgment. Let Your law be his guide. When sharp criticisms and accusations are made against him, strengthen his will to receive them. Thus he will receive help from wise reproof and ignore all unfounded accusations. Keep his mind ever alert to recognize Your law as his law. In Christ's name I pray.

Psalm 30:5

Weeping may go on all night, but in the morning there is joy.

Prayer

Dear Lord, thank You that each day gives us a new opportunity to love and worship You and start afresh with joy and hope. I pray our President will meet each day with renewed hope for the accomplishment of the tasks of his office. Each day may he feel strong and confident as he remembers "God is our refuge and strength – a very present help in time of trouble." Even when there has been weeping and disappointment at the end of a day, may he know that the next day may be one of unlimited possibilities through You, our gracious Lord. In Christ's name I pray.

My Concerns Today

_____

_____

_____

_____

My Concerns Today

_____

_____

_____

_____

Malachi 3:18

Then you will see the difference be-tween God's treatment of good men and bad, between those who serve Him and those who don't.

Prayer

Dear Lord, we know it is impossible for us to be truly good because none is good but You, our Lord and our God. But we pray for obedience of ourselves and our President. Only when each of us is obedient can we please You. When one can say as Mary did "I am the Lord's servant, and I am willing to do whatever He wants," can one become the instrument of God which God desires that one to be. Mold us, each citizen, O Lord, as well as our President, into useful and surrendered vessels for Your kingdom. In Christ's name I pray.

My Concerns Today

_____

_____

_____

_____

Luke 2:32,35

He is the light that will shine upon the nations. He will be the greatest joy of many others. And the deepest thoughts of many hearts shall be revealed.

Prayer

Dear Lord, our nation was founded for the freedom to worship You. But now our children and youth throughout our country cannot pray together in the public school classrooms of America. Please, O Lord, place upon our President's heart this need for a change to be made. May he be led by Your Holy Spirit to let Your Light shine upon our youth again. Let the people of our nation rise up and express the deep yearnings of our hearts for a mighty return to the faith of our founding fathers. In Christ's name I pray.

My Concerns Today

_____

_____

_____

_____

October 11

Hebrews 11:1

What is faith? It is the confident assurance that something we want is going to happen.

Prayer

Dear Lord, may our President this day have a confident and abiding assurance that he is ordained and chosen as leader of this nation. May the many promises Your Word has given us strengthen his faith in Your divine guidance. Give him that needed faith, O Lord. In Christ's name I pray.

My Concerns Today

_____

_____

_____

_____

October 12

Ephesians 5:17-18

Try to find out and do what the Lord wants you to...be filled with the Holy Spirit, and controlled by Him.

Prayer

Dear Lord God, give to our President this day renewed grace to understand that the world he cannot see is the real world. Though the life he lives today is in time – that of the 21st century – the issues with which he deals are eternal. His business interest for this nation and for the world must of necessity be secular in nature, but these issues must be based on his understanding of God's eternal values. O Lord, our President's responsibilities are great and opportunities to serve You can be found within them. For these opportunities and Your guidance we praise You. In Christ's name I pray.

My Concerns Today

_____

_____

_____

_____

October 13

Ephesians 3:15-16

When I think of the wisdom and scope of His plan, I fall down on my knees and pray to the Father of all the great family of God – that out of His glorious unlimited resources He will give you the mighty inner strengthening of His Holy Spirit.

Prayer

Dear Lord, God of heaven and earth, the scope of Your plan for our nation and for our President is beyond my understanding. You are so wise and so great and Your glorious resources are so unlimited. My soul bows down in humble prayer for our President's inner man to be lifted up in confidence and strength. I know You will endow him with unlimited courage and patience to perform the acts of leadership You require of him. In Christ's name I pray.

My Concerns Today

_____

_____

_____

October 14

Deuteronomy 16:20

Justice must prevail. That is the only way you will be successful in the land which the Lord your God is giving you.

Prayer

Dear Lord, You gave us Your Son that we might be saved and You are a loving and just God. You expect and demand justice from each of us. Your Word tells us "justice must prevail." O Lord, help our President find new ways for the employment of more people who need and want work. Let Your Spirit of justice and righteousness control the thinking and actions of government officials and leaders of business and industry that our unemployed may be employed. In Christ's name I pray for our President and the unemployed.

My Concerns Today

_____

_____

_____

Colossians 3:17

Whatever you do or say, let it be as a representative of the Lord Jesus, and come with Him into the presence of God, the Father, to give Him your thanks.

Prayer

Dear Lord God, to whom we belong, whether we are seeking understanding, prosperity, and harmony in our affairs, or blessings for others, we know progress is taking place. For all the words and deeds of the President to bring about Your Holy will in every area of our national life, we thank You, O Lord. You are our constant Mediator with Your Father, our God. In His holy presence we now praise Him for that which He is doing through the earnest work of our President. In Christ's name.

2 Corinthians 3:18

We Christians have no veil over our faces; we can be mirrors that brightly reflect the glory of the Lord. And as the Spirit of the Lord works within us, we become more and more like Him.

Prayer

Dear Father, we thank You for our Lord and Savior, Who works within us to do Your good will. We pray that our President may faithfully reflect the Spirit of our Savior in his personal behavior and in his decision-making. O Lord, renew the faith of our fathers in the people of our nation. As each glorifies the Christ through the reflection of Him in our daily lives, may we move our nation ever forward toward Your goals for our people. In Christ's name and for His glory, I pray.

My Concerns Today

_____
_____
_____
_____

My Concerns Today

_____
_____
_____
_____

Mark 11:24

Listen to me! You can pray for anything, and if you believe you have it, it's yours!

Prayer

Dear Lord, our Father and our God, who has all power on earth and in heaven, we praise You. Knowing You are all-powerful – knowing You love all nations – knowing You are gracious to forgive sins – hear, O Lord, the prayers of our President. As he prays in faith I pray with him for Your forgiveness, for Your guidance of our national leaders, and for decisions that will be in line with Your holy will. Now for the privilege of prayer, and for the faith that You hear and answer, I thank You, as I pray in Christ's name.

My Concerns Today

_____
_____
_____
_____

Psalm 55:17

I will pray morning, noon, and night, pleading aloud with God; and He will hear and answer.

Prayer

Dear Lord God, You have heard the prayers of the faithful. You do hear the prayers of Your people today. You always will hear the prayers of the penitent and obedient. I trust You daily to hear my prayers and those of the many who pray for our worthy President. We trust You to hear his prayers as he seeks Your guidance. Give it, O Lord. As he prays for knowledge and wisdom, endow him with full measure. As he pleads for patience, perseverance and perception, give the presence of Your Holy Spirit. In Christ's name I pray.

My Concerns Today

_____
_____
_____
_____

Matthew 22:37

Jesus replied, "Love the Lord your God with all your heart, soul, and mind."

Prayer

Dear Lord God, Jesus Christ has told us how we should love You – and this we are trying to do. Today I pray that our President will be reminded of this admonition – yea – this command of the Lord Jesus. And as he seeks to love You, our Father, with all his heart, may You receive the devotion of his heart, the adoration of his soul, and the obedience of his mind to Your glory. Through the President and his associates we pray for a special blessing of Your grace upon the affairs of our nation. In Christ's name I pray.

My Concerns Today

_____

_____

_____

_____

1 Peter 3:9

Don't repay evil for evil. Don't snap back at those who say unkind things about you. Instead, pray for God's help for them, for we are to be kind to others, and God will bless us for it.

Prayer

Dear Lord God, I pray for the President because he is in such a vulnerable position – where so many barbs, criticisms, words of ridicule, and maybe words of hatred will be hurled at him. O Lord, Your Word tells us You will bless those who pray for God's help. Our President does this. Your Word tells us to be kind to others. May our President be kind. May he show patience, kindness, gentleness toward others even in the most trying circumstances. Therefore, I ask Your special blessing upon him.

My Concerns Today

_____

_____

_____

_____

October 21

James 5:16

Pray for each other...the earnest prayer of a righteous man has great power and wonderful results.

Prayer

Dear Lord, bless our President as he gives of his faith to those who need renewed courage. As he visits and talks with the various citizens of different areas, bless him. As they share with one another the needs of the farmers and other areas of work, the goals and plans of the federal government to meet those needs, let all be strengthened. May they be encouraged by a mutual exchange of faith in You, our God, of faith in our economy, and of faith in one another. In Christ's name I pray.

My Concerns Today

October 22

Matthew 5:16

Let your good deeds glow for all to see, so that they will praise your heavenly Father.

Prayer

Dear Lord God, we know we are here for one purpose only – to praise our heavenly Father with our minds and hearts and glorify Him by the deeds of our lives. I pray this day that as our President visits with "the common man" – the unknown citizens – that Your Spirit will be so evident that all who meet and confer with him will be blessed. May the blessed Light of Your Spirit bless each and everyone. In Christ's name.

My Concerns Today

Lamentations 5:21

Turn us around and bring us back to You again. That is our only hope.

Prayer

Dear Lord God, Holy, Almighty, Creator and Redeemer, we praise You and magnify Your name. But there is great sin among us. You reject us when we sin. Though I pray for our President I realize that our people are bond slaves to the false gods of comfort, ease, and luxury. We have taught our youth to strive for wealth, power, and material success instead of lifting up before them the goals of service to humanity. We have not yet become color blind as to skin color. We forget that men are made in Your image. Forgive our sins, O Lord. In Christ's name I pray.

My Concerns Today

_____

_____

_____

_____

2 Timothy 1:7

For the Holy Spirit, God's gift, does not want you to be afraid of people, but to be wise and strong, and to love them and enjoy being with them.

Prayer

Dear Lord God, as I meditate upon Your loving Presence in the hearts of men, I praise Your holiness and goodness. May Your Presence abide in the mind and heart of our President this day and fill him with peace and courage. As he copes with outer events and circumstances may he still be able through all his conferences to affirm, "God has given me a courageous, confident, all-conquering spirit. I have the ability to act with confidence. I have a courageous spirit which knows no defeat when I follow the guidance of my Lord." In Christ's name I pray.

My Concerns Today

_____

_____

_____

_____

2 Corinthians 2:15

As far as God is concerned there is a sweet, wholesome fragrance in our lives. It is the fragrance of Christ within us.

Prayer

Dear Lord, You are so loving, so gracious, so powerful. I beseech You in the name of our Savior to bless the President with this fragrance of Christ. May this wholesome fragrance be recognized by all who see and hear him. In all his conferences and meetings with other leaders, may he exhibit godly wisdom and integrity. In Christ's name I pray.

Psalm 91:14-15

For the Lord says, "Because he loves Me, I will rescue him; I will make him great because he trusts in My name. When he calls on Me I will answer; I will be with him in trouble, and rescue him and honor him."

Prayer

Dear Lord God, who gave the words of life, hope, praise and promise to all the writers of the Book of Life, we praise You for this promise of protection. We thank You that our President is surrounded and enfolded in Your protective love; we can trust You to bring harmony, order, and safe conditions to this nation of Yours through Your guidance and protection of him. In Christ's name I pray.

My Concerns Today

_____

_____

_____

_____

My Concerns Today

_____

_____

_____

_____

Proverbs 9:9-10

Teach a wise man, and he will be the wiser; teach a good man and he will learn more. For the reverence and fear of God are basic to all wisdom. Knowing God results in every other kind of understanding.

Prayer

Dear Lord, I approach Your throne of grace, again, in behalf of our President. Make him a man who reverences You. He has learned well that a wise man practices self-control – even when taunted and ridiculed. Forgive those who treat him with such disrespect and bless him as he responds with gentle and understanding words. This reveals he lives under the control of Christ and practices the self control and forgiveness of a true disciple. Heavenly Father, in Christ's name, I thank You.

My Concerns Today

_____
_____
_____
_____

Proverbs 11:17

Your own soul is nourished when you are kind; it is destroyed when you are cruel.

Proverbs 12:18

Some people like to make cutting remarks, but the words of the wise soothe and heal.

Prayer

Dear Lord, You have given such control to our President that he does not respond in like manner, but in kindness and wisdom he speaks words which soothe and heal. O Lord, teach us to deal justly and respectfully with one another. We do not gain by cruel remarks, but lose the respect of others. Your Spirit gives our President power to return good for evil. For this Spirit in him, we praise You. In Christ's name I pray.

My Concerns Today

_____
_____
_____
_____

Isaiah 26:7-8

But for good men, the path is not uphill and rough! God does not give them a rough and treacherous path, but smoothes the road before them. O Lord, we love to do your will! Our heart's desire is to glorify Your name.

Prayer

Dear Lord, God of our fathers, God of all nations, God of all people, we magnify and praise Your name. As I pray for our President at this time, it is with a deep awareness that only You, our Lord, can smooth his path. Only Your power and goodness can make his path passable. Many do love to do Your will and I believe our President is such a person. May his heart's desire always be to glorify Your name. In Christ's name I pray.

My Concerns Today

_____

_____

_____

_____

Habakkuk 2:3

But these things I plan won't happen right away. Slowly, steadily, surely, the time approaches when the vision will be fulfilled. If it seems slow, do not despair, for these things will surely come to pass. Just be patient. They will not be overdue a single day!

Prayer

Dear Lord, Creator and Instigator of all men's dreams of good, we praise You for the unfolding of Your plans for our nation through the leadership of our President. Teach each of our leaders patience, O Lord. Teach them to have confidence in Your guidance, making them coworkers with You, in the realization of each vision and each dream which originated with You. For our President and for our nation I pray in Christ's name.

My Concerns Today

_____

_____

_____

_____

October 31

Isaiah 40:31

But they that wait upon the Lord shall renew their strength. They shall mount up with wings like eagles; they shall run and not be weary; they shall walk and not faint.

Prayer

Dear Lord, lift up our President in spirit and in truth and prove to all who pray and believe that Your mighty power is still supreme. Let him be renewed as the eagle whose wings are made strong because of the altitude in which he must fly. Lift our President up to higher levels of communion with You that his eyes may not be dimmed by the smog of present day confusion. Place his feet on higher ground than party politics. Let his mind see world needs, not just national needs. Renew him, O Lord, for Christ's sake.

My Concerns Today

_____

_____

_____

_____

1 Peter 3:15

Quietly trust yourself to Christ your Lord and if anybody asks why you believe as you do, be ready to tell him, and do it in a gentle and respectful way.

Prayer

Dear Lord, we thank You for our President. We realize he has great responsibilities. I pray this day that You will give him a clear understanding in his mind and heart of who he is in the Kingdom of God. I pray he will be able to explain what he believes whenever opportunity is given him. May his statements always bring honor and glory to Your name. In Christ's name.

1 Thessalonians 5:8

But let us who live in the light, keep sober, protected by the armor of faith and love and wearing as our helmet the happy hope of salvation.

Prayer

Dear Lord, who has established the family form of life, bless our President as a father, head of a household. Send Your heavenly blessing upon every member of his household. Let Christ rule in every heart and His law be honored by every member of the White House staff. As they live and work there, may they not only help one another in their faith, but may they grow daily in spirit and in the truly good life which You desire for all Your children. In Christ's name and for His glory, I pray.

My Concerns Today

_____

_____

_____

_____

My Concerns Today

_____

_____

_____

_____

1 Samuel 10:7

From that time on your decisions should be based on whatever seems best under the circumstances, for the Lord will guide you.

Prayer

Dear Lord God, just as in the days when Samuel directed Saul to do what You guided him to do, so today we trust You to guide our President. In his position no one can make decisions for him. You alone have the wisdom for the right decision under the present circumstances. You alone know how to use the people around our President for Your purposes. Bless each and every one of them. Keep us firmly fixed in the faith of Christ. Teach us patience, O Lord. In Christ's name I pray.

My Concerns Today

_____
_____
_____
_____

Psalm 31:19

Oh, how great is Your goodness to those who publicly declare that You will rescue them. For You have stored up great blessings for those who trust and reverence You.

Prayer

Dear Lord God, how great is Your goodness! How blessed is Your peace! How constant is Your care! How wise Your guidance! For all these magnificent evidences of Your power and Your love, we thank You. May our President publicly declare his belief in and his love for You and Your Son. I claim for him the great blessings which Your Holy Word tells us are stored up for Your children. In every trial and tribulation may he trust You. In Christ's name I pray.

My Concerns Today

_____
_____
_____
_____

Matthew 6:8

Remember, your Father knows exactly what you need even before you ask Him.

Prayer

Dear Lord, You always know our needs before we bring them to You. But we are taught that You want us to ask You, nevertheless. For our President, I beseech Your grace – all these, my dear Lord - the grace of a thankful heart; the grace of courage in controversy and in danger; the grace of a boldness to stand for what is right; the grace of bodily discipline; the grace of charity to abstain from hasty judgment; the grace of strict truthfulness; the grace to endure disappointments with hope; the grace of steadfastness to endure with confidence, knowing You are in control. In Christ's name I pray.

My Concerns Today

_____

_____

_____

_____

Ezekiel 36:27

And I will put My Spirit within you, so that you will obey My laws and do whatever I command.

Prayer

Dear Lord, we know You are not only the Almighty God, and Creator of the Universe, but You are a personal God. You are our Father in heaven. We are sons and daughters of Yours through Christ. As a personal God, no one can know what You command of each of Your children. Our President stands alone in his relationship with You as his Father and his God. He receives Your personal commands. Help him to obey You always no matter what the worldly obstacles may be which stand in his way. In Christ's name I pray.

My Concerns Today

_____

_____

_____

_____

Luke 4:32

For He spoke as one who knew the truth, instead of merely quoting the opinion of others as His authority.

Prayer

Dear Lord, only You and Your Word are the Source of Truth. To know You is to know the truth, and from that, draw the confidence one needs in human confrontations of political and social problems. I believe, O Lord, that is because Your Truth enables our President to make his judgments and express his own thoughts. You are his authority. Thank You. Continue to guide and sustain our President for Christ's sake. In His name I pray.

John 4:34

My nourishment comes from doing the will of God who sent Me.

Prayer

Dear Father God, as we read and meditate upon these words of our Lord Jesus Christ, we praise and adore You. He was a perfect and obedient Son. Your will was His law while He was here on earth. His total life and will were under Your control. May our President be a true follower of the Lord Jesus proclaiming by word and deed "My nourishment comes from doing the will of God." I pray that through Your divine guidance, O Lord, our President will be led. In Christ's name I pray.

My Concerns Today

_____

_____

_____

_____

My Concerns Today

_____

_____

_____

_____

Psalm 104:24

O Lord, what a variety You have made and in wisdom You have made them all! The earth is full of Your riches.

Prayer

Dear Lord, as our President and our Congress work on each bill, bless and guide them. Let them realize anew that You have placed on the earth Your children who have needs; You have placed within the earth and sea means of meeting those needs; and You have made man in Your image. You will direct their minds into new areas of thought – creative thought – if their minds are loosed from selfish interests and freed to receive Your thoughts. May Your will be done for the good of all. In Christ's name and for His glory, I pray.

My Concerns Today

_____
_____
_____
_____

Romans 4:20-21

He believed God, for his faith and trust grew ever stronger and he praised God for this blessing even before it happened. He was completely sure God was able to do anything He promised.

Prayer

Dear Lord, as Abraham believed, had faith, and trusted You to keep Your promise, and to do what was "impossible," so teach us to trust and believe. Especially bless our President with belief in the impossible. His dreams for many good things for this nation and the world seem impossible. But nothing, O Lord, is impossible with You. Abraham at 100 and Sarah at 90 having a baby? "Impossible" said man. "Possible" said God. Thank You for your "impossibles." Grant some to our nation. In Christ's name I pray.

My Concerns Today

_____
_____
_____
_____

Nahum 1:7

The Lord is good. When trouble comes He is the place to go! And He knows everyone who trusts in Him!

Prayer

Dear Lord, who loves each of us so much more than we can love one another, draw near to our President at this early morning hour and strengthen him for the duties of the day. If he is sad or discouraged, let him realize anew that You are with him. Let Your Spirit convince him that he can trust You to supply all his needs – to go on ahead to open doors for the solution of our acute national problems. Many of Your children are praying, O Lord. Hear our prayers. In Christ's name I pray.

1 Corinthians 1:3

May God our Father and the Lord Jesus Christ give you all of His blessings, and great peace of heart and mind.

Prayer

Dear Lord, how comforting it is for Your children to read such blessings as this one written by Your servant, Paul, to the Christians at Corinth. Just as, through sharing, joys are multiplied and sorrows are lessened, so in Christian fellowship blessings expressed bless both giver and recipient. Though our President does not know me, O Lord I pray that he is a follower of Yours and so I pray that the blessing of God, the Father, and our Savior, Jesus Christ, be upon him this day and always. In Christ's name I pray.

My Concerns Today

_____
_____
_____
_____

My Concerns Today

_____
_____
_____
_____

1 Corinthians 2:10

But we know about these things because God has sent His Spirit to tell us, and His Spirit searches out and shows us all of God's deepest secrets.

Prayer

Dear Lord God, send Your Spirit daily into the mind and heart of our President to remind him of Your authority, Your grace, Your power and Your love. Your promises bind You to us forever because You cannot lie. We thank You for Your blessed promises: "Come unto Me…and I will give you rest." "I shall be with you always even unto the end of the world." "My grace is sufficient." "Ask and it shall be given you." "I have chosen you." "The steps of good men are directed by the Lord." "All who seek for God shall live in joy." "The Lord is faithful to His promises." Thank You, Father.

My Concerns Today

_____

_____

_____

_____

Psalm 136:16

Praise Him who led His people through the wilderness, for His loving kindness continues forever.

Prayer

Dear Lord God, as You led the Israelites of Old Testament history through the wilderness, so You have led the people of our nation. Always You have used leaders to found our nation, to write its famous documents, to wage war for those ideals we hold dear, to free the slaves, to fight in other lands for rights for all people, to cultivate the land that more people might be fed, to seek for and to use scientific means to conquer diseases. So, now I pray for Your Holy Spirit to imbue our President with gifts to accomplish all You have in mind.

My Concerns Today

_____

_____

_____

_____

Psalm 53:2

God looks down from heaven, searching among all mankind to see if there is a single one who does right and really seeks for God.

Prayer

Dear Lord, look down upon our President and see him as only You can see him – the inner man – and cleanse him from every sin or weakness that would impede him on his journey. Renew a right and holy spirit within him for the work You would have him do. Bless each international leader with whom our President deals. Let their dealings with one another come under Your holy gaze and be found pleasing in Your sight. In Christ's name and for His glory I pray.

My Concerns Today

_____

_____

_____

_____

Psalm 33:18

But the eyes of the Lord are watching over those who fear Him, who rely upon His steady love.

Prayer

Dear Lord, we are relying upon Your steady love to bless America, where so many of Your children faithfully worship You, where many of our national leaders are true followers of Your Son, Jesus Christ. We believe Your eyes are watching over our President and our country to protect and to guide him and us. We believe, we trust and we thank You. In Christ's name I pray, believing.

My Concerns Today

_____

_____

_____

_____

Psalm 25:14

Friendship with God is reserved for those who reverence Him. With them alone He shares the secrets of His promises.

Prayer

Dear Lord, You have created us with the free choice of making decisions as we desire. I pray for our President to be wise in every decision he makes today regarding his duties as our President. May he seek Your divine wisdom and guidance. I know You, Lord, have great plans for America because we acknowledge You created our nation for Your purposes. In Christ's name.

Psalm 20:7-8

Some nations boast of armies and of weaponry, but our boast is in the Lord, our God. Those nations will collapse and perish; we will arise to stand firm and sure.

Prayer

Dear Lord, how I pray that our nation will not continue to boast of our greatness in terms of armies and armaments but rather in our commitment to You, our Lord and our God. As our President seeks to communicate to other nations his idea of human rights, bless him with astuteness of mind, graciousness of spirit and clarity of speech. Turn our minds away from weaponry as strength, O Lord, and fill our minds with Your greatness and goodness which are available as our allies, if we love and worship You. In Christ's name I pray.

My Concerns Today

_____
_____
_____
_____

My Concerns Today

_____
_____
_____
_____

Psalm 110:3,5

And your strength shall be renewed day by day like morning dew….God stands beside you to protect you.

Prayer

Dear Lord, You have promised through the Psalmist and Your Holy Spirit that our President's strength will be renewed day by day. We thank you for that promise. Then through the same Psalmist You have promised to protect him. We thank You for that promise. We are told that You feed those who trust You and therefore, I feel free to speak to You as a loving follower of Your Son, asking You to "feed" in every way necessary, our President. He needs to be "fed" by Your Holy Spirit in an understanding and in wisdom that he may successfully play his part in human affairs. In Christ's name and for His sake, I pray.

My Concerns Today

_____

_____

_____

_____

Psalm 21:7

And because the king trusts in the Lord, he will never stumble, never fall; for he depends upon the steadfast love of the God who is above all gods.

Prayer

Dear Lord, may our President of this great nation trust in You and follow You with steadfast faith. May You so govern his life that he may reflect You in every decision he has to make. We know You are the God above all gods. You are the God of Abraham, Isaac and Jacob. In Christ's name.

My Concerns Today

_____

_____

_____

_____

Micah 4:3

He will arbitrate among the nations and dictate to strong nations far away. They will beat their swords into plowshares and their spears into pruning hooks, nations shall no longer fight each other, for all war will end.

Prayer

Dear Lord, I thank You today for our President. He does have a powerful position of leadership – not only in America but in the world. Give him wisdom and give him grace in all international conferences. Let our country, O Lord, bring honor to Your Holy Name. In Christ's name.

My Concerns Today

_____
_____
_____
_____

Psalm 121:5-8

Jehovah Himself is caring for you. He is your defender. He protects you day and night. He keeps you from all evil and preserves your life. He keeps His eye upon you as you come and go, and always guards you.

Prayer

Dear Lord, we know that Your love encompasses all Your children. We realize that if You, as our Father, know every sparrow that falls and clothe every lily of the field, then surely You know every need of our President and You are guiding and protecting him. And for all this we thank You. In the blessed name of Jesus Christ, I pray.

My Concerns Today

_____
_____
_____
_____

November 23

Micah 7:15

"Yes," replies the Lord, "I will do mighty miracles for you, like those when I brought you out of slavery in Egypt."

Prayer

Dear Lord, as we read Your Word and hear the prophecies of Your prophets, we see You at work in the changing of the world. Our President has been chosen by You through the voice of the people to be our leader. Therefore I pray You will make him Your instrument of peace as he is needed by any or all the leaders of other nations. Make him wise as You know wisdom. Make him patient as You are patient. Fill him with Your great compassion for humanity and make him amenable to Your guidance. In Christ's name I pray.

November 24

Psalm 21:13

Accept our praise, O Lord, for all Your glorious power.

Prayer

Dear Lord God, we have so much to thank You for. On this day we thank You for those who founded our country where we would be free to worship You. We thank You for those who have died for us and for leaders who have had vision, courage, and perseverance in bringing this country to its present state of technical, scientific and industrial development. Most of all, Father, we thank You for the righteous people of our nation and for Your leadership. Now thank You this day for our President. Bless him and his family bountifully this day. In Christ's name I pray.

My Concerns Today

_____

_____

_____

_____

My Concerns Today

_____

_____

_____

_____

Psalm 25:21-22

Assign me godliness and integrity as my bodyguards, for I expect You to protect me and to ransom Israel from all her troubles.

Prayer

Dear Lord, how wise and noble are these requests for a leader of any nation! As God assigns godliness and integrity to His emissary, then verily that nation may be so led as to actually save it from dire disaster. Therefore I pray for our President to be protected by You through the virtues of character You have assigned to him. May America be ransomed from her tremendous problems of unemployment, crime, educational upheaval, widespread disease, child abuse and neglect of the practice of holy habits. In Christ's name and for His glory I pray.

My Concerns Today

_____

_____

_____

_____

Proverbs 3:21-23

Have two goals: wisdom — that is, knowing and doing right — and common sense. Don't let them slip away, for they fill you with living energy… They keep you safe from defeat and disaster and from stumbling off the trail.

Prayer

Dear Lord, may our President seek Your wisdom because he wants to do right at all times. Help him, O Lord, to be a sensible man who listens patiently and impartially to people of varying opinions. According to Your Word, Lord God, You will fill him with energy. Keep him from stumbling off the trail. In Christ's name I pray.

My Concerns Today

_____

_____

_____

_____

1 Corinthians 11:7, 11

God's glory is man made in His image, and man's glory is the woman. But remember that in God's plan men and women need each other.

Prayer

Dear Lord God, since You ordained from the beginning that man should have a woman to help him, we thank You that our President has been so blessed. We thank You for the life, the talents, the charm, the dedication to duty of his wife. When You took bone from Adam's side and made Eve, You showed us that woman was not to be above or below man but was to take her place by his side, as his partner and his helpmate. Bless our First Lady and our President as they work side by side for our country and Your kingdom. In Christ's name I pray.

My Concerns Today

_____

_____

_____

_____

Proverbs 1:7

How does a man become wise? The first step is to trust and reverence the Lord!

Prayer

Dear Lord, knowing that our Father God is all wise, we can trust Him to give to each of us the wisdom we need. Right now I ask for that wisdom for the President. Knowing our heavenly Father has all means for meeting each physical need we have, I ask those blessings for our President. Knowing that trust and reverence are gifts sent by the Holy Spirit to those who desire fellowship with the Father, I ask now for those blessed gifts to be bestowed on him this day and always. In Your Holy name I pray.

My Concerns Today

_____

_____

_____

_____

Psalm 147:4-5

He counts the stars and calls them all by name. How great He is! His power is absolute! His understanding is unlimited.

Prayer

Dear God Almighty, as we enter the Advent season, when all the world looks toward the holy act of God which created a Savior for mankind, we bow our soul in reverence. Yes, Your power is absolute! Your understanding is unlimited! But even though You, O God, have such knowledge that You count the stars and call them by name, You also know each of us and call us by name. Through the presence of Your Holy Spirit, enlighten our President this day, O Lord, and reveal Yourself anew to his soul. In Christ's name I pray.

My Concerns Today

_____
_____
_____
_____

Proverbs 10:8

The wise man is glad to be instructed, but a self-sufficient fool falls flat on his face.

Prayer

Dear Lord, our President is a wise man. He wants to be instructed. He has many advisors. Please, dear Lord, bless each person who advises with him daily. Bend them to Your will, O Lord, that they may be Your channels through which You advise our President. As he prepares for any trip to other nations, may his mind be enlightened with the knowledge of how he may best confer with each leader. May Your Spirit so pervade his spirit that he will be a true messenger of Your Spirit while he represents our nation in these international relationships. In Christ's name I pray.

My Concerns Today

_____
_____
_____
_____

Philippians 1:23

Sometimes I want to live and at other times I don't, for I long to go and be with Christ.

Prayer

Dear Lord, just as Paul felt at times that he would like to give up the battle for souls, so our President may grow weary of the constant struggle. All Christians long to be with Christ where there will be no struggles, no heartaches, no failures. But we all have promises to keep and miles to go. Our President wants to keep his promises. Therefore, I claim the promise of Your Word for him this day and always that You will give him the strength and wisdom to keep every promise and to travel every difficult mile. In Christ's name I pray.

My Concerns Today

———————————————
———————————————
———————————————
———————————————

John 15:10-11

When you obey Me you are living in My love, just as I obey My Father and live in His love. I have told you so that you will be filled with My joy.

Prayer

Dear Lord God, Christians who are unhappy have not yet grasped the secret that if Christ dwells in our hearts and we allow Him control, we are filled with joy in living for You. May our President radiate this joy that accompanies such an obedience to You and love for Christ. As he speaks to the press, we notice his calm control and optimistic attitude about the most serious affairs of government. Thank You for his inner joy which is due to Your residence in him. Keep him sensitive to the subtle wooing and guidance of our Savior, in whose blessed name I pray.

My Concerns Today

———————————————
———————————————
———————————————
———————————————

Luke 14:27

And no one can be My disciple who does not carry his own cross and follow Me.

Prayer

Dear Lord, we often misunderstand the "carrying of a cross" and mistake the suffering which all members of the human race bear simply because we are mortal. Surely Christ understood and bore all such suffering and pain in teaching us how to live. When He told us to take up our cross and follow Him, He meant for us to choose to suffer with Him for a divine purpose. Our President has chosen the cross of heavy national and international responsibility and service in his following of our Lord. Therefore, I ask You, O God, this day give him Your divine blessing. In Christ's name I pray.

My Concerns Today

_____

_____

_____

_____

Matthew 19:26

But with God, everything is possible.

Prayer

Dear Lord, there are so many things expected of our President which defy reason. No doubt he wants to make it possible for all people to work who want to work. He wants to stabilize our Medicare system. He wants to help the farmers. He wants to raise the moral standards of our people. He wants to increase our national product. He wants to lower the cost of medical care. Oh, so many advantages for our people are his dreams, but they are impossible unless You make them possible. Help him, O Lord, to do the "impossible." In Christ's name I pray.

My Concerns Today

_____

_____

_____

_____

Mark 8:11

"Do a miracle for us," they said.

Prayer

Dear Lord, so often we forget, as did Christ's apostles, that You have given us miracle after miracle, and yet we ask for more. Forgive us, Father, when instead of thanking You for each step of progress which You have made possible, we still beg for more. Let us, with our President, give thanks and praise to You, the Creator of all people. Let us pray that all nations will work toward peace. Bless our President when and if they call upon him for help. In Christ's name I pray.

Proverbs 30:5

Every word of God proves true. He defends all who come to Him for protection.

Prayer

Dear Lord, our President needs Your protection at all times. Physical dangers lurk around those in positions of leadership. Send Your protecting angel to safeguard him at home and abroad. His mind needs protection against the enemies of fear, distress, doubt, and discouragement. Send Your special angels O Lord, to keep him from becoming a victim of such enemies. His spirit needs renewal daily because the demands upon him are so great. Be in him the spirit of light, life, and health, O Lord. In Christ's name I pray.

My Concerns Today

_____
_____
_____
_____

My Concerns Today

_____
_____
_____
_____

1 Corinthians 3:22-23

He has given you the whole world to use…all are yours, and you belong to Christ and Christ is God's.

Prayer

Dear Father God, You have given to our President the whole world to use. You are the Creator and therefore it would seem that You have authority over all Your creation. But You gave Christ authority over all of it, and our President belongs to Christ. Thus we know that through grace You have made him a joint-heir with Christ of all that belongs to You. I pray You will make him thoroughly aware that he may draw any treasures he wishes to use for mankind, from the great storehouse of the King of Kings. In Christ's name I pray.

My Concerns Today

_____
_____
_____
_____

Exodus 20:3

Thou shalt have no other gods before Me.

Prayer

Dear Lord, You have so plainly told us that we shall not worship false gods. We have all failed You so often. We pray to You for pardon and forgiveness. If our President is so tempted to place some false god of self-interest before adherence to his worship of You, forgive him. Make him aware, O Lord, that he has compromised. The two laws of faith and of compromise confront him every day. Each day we are called upon to believe or to doubt. Satan whispers to us to compromise that we may get what we want. But, You, our Lord, tell us to trust and obey, to have faith. Dear Lord, help our President to stand on faith, and never compromise.

My Concerns Today

_____
_____
_____
_____

December 9

Romans 8:38

For I am convinced that nothing can ever separate us from His love. Death can't and life can't.

Prayer

Dear Lord, no matter where our President may go this day – no matter where duty calls him we know that You are there. Nothing can separate You from us. Your love is everywhere, available at all times, visible in all circumstances, abiding in the God-nature of every man. At this moment I pray for this magnificent awareness of You to be present in the mind and heart of our President. In his awareness let his human will be filled with complete submission to Your holy and divine will for the glory of the Christ, in whose name I pray.

My Concerns Today

_____

_____

_____

_____

December 10

Psalm 42:5

Why be discouraged and sad? Hope in God...Yes, I shall again praise Him for His help.

Prayer

Dear Lord, whatever experiences of discouragement or lack of accomplishment, or feelings of inadequacy our President may have felt yesterday, erase them this day by awaking in him Your excellent gift of hope: hope of accomplishment of tasks too heavy for human hands or heart; hope for a love that will encompass all people, varying in color, creed, and custom; hope for a heart and mind able to appreciate, enjoy, and use all the bounties of nature. But, O Lord, our hope in God is the fulfillment of all these hopes. Bless our President with this hope. In Christ's name I pray.

My Concerns Today

_____

_____

_____

_____

Psalm 82:8

Stand up, O God, and judge the earth. For all of it belongs to You. All nations are in Your hands.

Prayer

Dear Lord, here in the quietness of Your Presence I pray with the Psalmist of old, the earth does belong to You and all nations are in Your hands. You have made every beauty of the earth. You have created every man. You have fashioned every creature and every person for Your own purposes. Now I pray that in each area of our President's being, he may feel the all-pervading spirit of power and love which flow only from the Source of all perfection. Your power reigns supreme, O God, and only those who know it are wise. In Christ's name I pray.

My Concerns Today

_____
_____
_____
_____

Isaiah 30:15

For the Lord God, the Holy One of Israel, says: Only in returning to Me and waiting for Me will you be saved; in quietness and confidence is your strength.

Prayer

Dear Lord, as Christian people, we believe in quietness and confidence as strength. And we pray for them for our President. We know that only in returning to You and waiting for You can he have perfect peace. As God spoke to the Hebrews through Isaiah, may He speak to our President through every instrument You use today. Bless the leaders of other nations, and others in our government's service as they report situations to our President. May he receive them with understanding, a gift of Your Holy Spirit. In Christ's name I pray.

My Concerns Today

_____
_____
_____
_____

Acts 17:26

He created all the people of the world from one man, Adam, and scattered the nations across the face of the earth.

Prayer

Dear Lord, when our President travels from nation to nation, grant him the wisdom to see Your love and truth in the most unexpected places. Help our President to share Your concern for all nations and all people. May all of us, who are Your children, cooperate in the achievement of Your holy purposes for all men. I pray, dear Lord, for Your protecting angels to guard him from bodily harm. May Your Spirit of truth invade his mind and give him new understandings. Let Your spirit of love energize his total being as he relates to the needs of the nations. In Christ's name I pray.

My Concerns Today

_____
_____
_____
_____

Philippians 4:8

…Fix your thoughts on what is true and good and right…

Prayer

Dear Lord, as I pray for our President at this time, I think of what a great gift You bestowed upon us in the gift of thought. I want to thank You especially this day for all the thought processes he will engage in today. Whatever is true, honorable, just, lovely, and gracious, let him think on these things. In every situation and in every person, there will be something worthy of praise. In all advice, interpretations and warnings brought to him this day, make his mind able to cull out the worthy and the true for wise use. In all the pleas for help, for mercy, and for justice, let his mind be receptive. In Christ's name and for His glory I pray.

My Concerns Today

_____
_____
_____
_____

2 Timothy 1:9

It is He who saved us and chose us for His holy work, not because we deserved it but because that was His plan long before the world began.

Prayer

Dear Lord, our praise and all honor are due You, for You have saved us and then chosen each of us to follow You, to serve You, to love You. None of us deserves these special gifts. They are ours not because of our worthiness, but for God's holy plan. Long before the world began, You had the plan for our President in Your hand. How great You are, our Father! How great Your power! How great Your love! Some men fight. Some work for peace. Some destroy. Others build. Dear Lord, I pray that our President will be the man You planned for him to be. Guide him in every way.

My Concerns Today

_____

_____

_____

_____

Hebrews 12:25

So see to it that you obey Him who is speaking to you…How terrible our danger if we refuse to listen to God who speaks to us from heaven.

Prayer

Dear Lord, how true it is that God speaks to us and He has various ways of doing it. I'm sure You are speaking to our President every day. I pray he will listen and will recognize Your voice. The plans You have for world peace and the ways in which our President and our country should help will be made clear to him. Help him to listen and obey. As leaders from other nations seek counsel with our President, be present in their midst and guide their thinking. In Christ's name I pray.

My Concerns Today

_____

_____

_____

_____

James 1:2-3

Dear brothers, is your life full of difficulties and temptations? Then be happy, for when the way is rough, your patience has a chance to grow.

Prayer

Dear Lord, as I pray for our President today, I include presidents of other nations. These represent nations of people so diversified in social, religious and cultural heritage that only by the grace of Your love can they come together and confer. They must reach new levels of understanding and of respect. They deeply desire to do so. Help them, O Lord. Only through Your divine guidance can they make progress toward permanent peace for their people. In Christ's name I pray.

Psalm 37:5

Commit everything you do to the Lord. Trust Him to help you do it and He will.

Prayer

Dear Lord God, our President has such great responsibilities that I pray he will commit everything he does to You. There are countless millions of people around the world praying for peace. So many of Your children are sick, hungry, homeless, and discouraged and they cry out for all war to end and peace to come. Bless our President as he fulfills his opportunity to be a peacemaker. I trust You, O Lord, to help him with that which he has committed unto You. In Christ's name, and for His glory I pray.

My Concerns Today

_____
_____
_____
_____

My Concerns Today

_____
_____
_____
_____

Proverbs 2:6,8

For the Lord grants wisdom! His every word is a treasure of knowledge and understanding. He grants good sense to the godly – His saints. He is their shield, protecting them and guarding their pathway.

Prayer

Dear Lord God, I pray You will flood the minds and hearts of our leaders with Your holy words of wisdom and truth. Give to our President a very special gift of wisdom regarding his words and attitudes. Let him reflect Your justice and concern for all mankind. Bless each member of his Cabinet and all members of his family that they may support him and meet his needs for advice and companionship during these critical days. In Christ's name I pray.

My Concerns Today

_____

_____

_____

_____

Job 12:13

But true wisdom and power are God's. He alone knows what we should do; He understands.

Prayer

Dear Lord God, may our President today have a deeper sense of security regarding decisions he must make. So I pray at this time that You will send him this gift of reassurance of Your concern and guidance. As a finite being, he cannot have the knowledge and wisdom You have. Give him the assurance that You are his Source of all the wisdom he needs. Let him take Your strong hand in his frail one, Lord, and take firmer steps because he feels Your strength. You alone, O God, know what our President should do under all circumstances. Keep him obedient to the Master in whose name I pray.

My Concerns Today

_____

_____

_____

_____

James 1:8

If you don't ask with faith, don't expect the Lord to give you any solid answer.

Prayer

Dear Lord, I come to you in faith, believing you are hearing my prayers and answering every one. Of course, Father, I know You may have to say "No" to some of my requests because You know what is best and right at all times. Or you may tell me to be patient and wait a while for Your answer. But I trust You and shall continue to pray for our President. You whisper to my heart: "Never criticize. I am in control. Be patient and wait for the solid answer which will surely come some day." Thank You, Father, for the comfort of Your holy Word which gives us the assurance. In Christ's name and for His glory, I pray.

My Concerns Today

_____
_____
_____
_____

Psalm 86:11

Tell me where you want me to go and I will go there. May every fiber of my being unite in reverence to your Name.

Prayer

Dear Father God, who is the Creator of the Universe and to whom we owe our entire being, hear my prayer of intercession for my President. May every fiber of this man, who was created by You, be filled with reverence for Your blessed name. Wherever You want him to go, may he be pleased to go. Whatever You want him to do, may he be overjoyed to do. Whenever You call upon him, may he be reverently attentive to Your gentle voice. In Christ's name and for His glory I pray.

My Concerns Today

_____
_____
_____
_____

Psalm 101:2

I will try to walk a blameless path, but how I need your help, especially in my own home, where I long to act as I should.

Prayer

Dear Lord, now as always our Guide and Counselor, as well as our Savior, be with our President in his home. During these Christmas holidays I pray for him and each member of his family to be blessed with a special sensitivity of the President's need for rest and quietness, and make no unnecessary demands upon him. In Christ's name I pray, for his entire family this Christmas season.

My Concerns Today

_____

_____

_____

_____

Joel 2:28

After I have poured out my rains again, I will pour out My Spirit upon all of you.

Prayer

Dear Lord God, who controls the Universe, who sends the sunshine and the rain, be with our President in spirit this day. As he talks with representatives from various areas of our country, bless him with understanding of their problems, patience with their legitimate unrest and a deep dependence upon Your guidance for solutions to these problems which exist. The economic conditions are so complex I cannot understand them. But I know You, my Father, and I trust You to help all our leaders, our farmers, and our country. In Christ's name I pray.

My Concerns Today

_____

_____

_____

_____

December 25

Luke 2:14

"Glory to God in the highest heaven," they sang, "and peace on earth for all those pleasing Him."

Prayer

Dear Father, our God and Creator of all men, today we praise and thank You for the birth of our Savior Jesus Christ. Just as the angels sang to the shepherds "Glory to God" and "peace on earth" we pray that this day more men than ever before shall sing the songs of praise and glory to God. I pray that our President may be pleasing our Lord as he and all others worship You this day. In Christ's name I pray.

December 26

Psalm 33:4

For all God's words are right, and everything He does is worthy of our trust.

Prayer

Dear Father God, how precious are the promises of Your Word. You told us to come to You in quietness and trust and You would renew our strength. On this day of rest after Christmas I pray for renewed strength for our President and blessings of family joy and peace. Through Your power of complete renewal of body, mind, and spirit, may he be refreshed for the new duties of the new year which he will encounter. In Christ's name, and for His glory I pray.

My Concerns Today

_____
_____
_____
_____

My Concerns Today

_____
_____
_____
_____

Psalm 119:165

Those who love Your laws have great peace of heart and mind and do not stumble.

Prayer

Dear Lord, Maker of heaven and earth, I beseech You to hear my prayer this day. As our President looks to You, the Source of all his needs, heighten his aspirations toward the achievement of Christian perfection. Increase the depth of his commitment to service. Expand ever wider his concern for humanity's welfare. Keep his eyes ever open to see the thread of Truth running through all aspects of life. In Christ's name I pray.

2 Timothy 3:12

Those who decide to please Christ Jesus by living godly lives will suffer at the hands of those who hate Him.

Prayer

Dear Lord, You gave us Your Son as a Savior. We thank You with all our hearts. Because He loved us so much, we want to please Christ by living godly lives. But those who hate Christ often persecute His followers. They do not understand You, our Father, nor Christ, the Savior. As I read about such critics of our President I pray for them. But, also, I ask of You, O Lord, to give to our President a sense of Your presence. Let him hear Your reassuring voice. Let him see evidences of Your loving provision. I pray in Christ's holy name and for His glory.

My Concerns Today

_____

_____

_____

_____

My Concerns Today

_____

_____

_____

_____

2 Corinthians 4:7

But this precious treasure – this light and power that now shine within us – is held in a perishable container, that is, in our weak bodies. Everyone can see that the glorious power within must be from God and is not our own.

Prayer

Dear Lord, Your Spirit gives light wherever it is allowed to shine. You are so glorious in the revelation of Your presence. May that light be revealed in the mind and spirit of our President. His calmness, poise, and humility are evident as he lets Your power live in him. Thank You, Father, that Your precious gifts of power and light are available to each of us. In Christ's name.

My Concerns Today

_____

_____

_____

_____

1 Corinthians 2:16

But strange as it may seem, we Christians actually do have within us a portion of the very thoughts and mind of Christ.

Prayer

Dear Lord God, Father of our Savior, Jesus Christ, how we praise You for this relationship Christians have, not only with our Savior, but with You. Because of this relationship existing between our President and You, I pray for him with perfect trust that wherever he is, You are there. With whomever he is conversing, You are there doing Your perfect work in him and through him because he has made himself available to You. Help all who pray for our President today to know they are channels through whom Your power flows. In Christ's name I pray.

My Concerns Today

_____

_____

_____

_____

December 31

Psalm 80:19

Turn us again to Yourself, O God of the armies of heaven. Look down on us, Your face aglow with joy and love – only then shall we be saved.

Prayer

Dear Lord of heaven and earth, we praise Your holy name for the miracles we have seen this year. Thank you for our President's knowledge of the Word, his commitment to Your divine purposes, his belief in government under God made reality by the practice of justice for all, and his faith that all men may come to You. All the nations are Yours, O God. Have Your way with Your servant, the President, that through him You may move Your peole nearer to that new Kingdom which is to come. In the name of the Savior of all mankind, I pray.

My Concerns Today

_____

_____

_____

_____

Index of Scriptures Used

SDG

Here are my directions:
Pray much for others; plead for God's mercy upon them;
give thanks for all He is going to do for them.
Pray in this way for kings and for all others who
are in authority over us, or are in places of high
responsibility, so that we can live in peace and quietness,
spending our time in godly living and
thinking much about the Lord.

1 Timothy 2:1-2

JOIN FREE!

Blessed is the nation whose God is the Lord.
Psalm 33:12a

THE PRESIDENTIAL PRAYER TEAM™

Mobilizing America to pray daily for the President, his Cabinet
and other leaders of our nation.

My family and I have been blessed by the prayers of countless Americans. We have felt their
sustaining power and we're incredibly grateful.
— President George W. Bush

A new chapter is being written in the history of our nation. Americans are experiencing a strong sense of unity and purpose, learning that earnest and fervent prayer on behalf of the nation genuinely moves the hand of God.

This has probably been one of the most positive changes I've made in my life over the
past year. With this prayer team, I am less frustrated over what is happening in and
with the government.
— Claudia (a *Presidential Prayer Team* member)

Through the efforts of *The Presidential Prayer Team*, Americans will learn that our nation was truly founded on biblical principles – that our Founding Fathers were men of prayer. America is recapturing our Christian heritage and taking back the ground that has been lost.

Direct my thoughts, words, and work, wash away my sins…and purge my heart by Thy Holy
Spirit…Daily frame me more and more into the likeness of Thy Son Jesus Christ.
— President George Washington

We all can pray. We all should pray. We should ask the fulfillment
of God's will. We should ask for courage, wisdom, for the quietness of
soul which comes alone to them who place their lives in His hands.
— President Harry S. Truman

[THE GOAL]

To mobilize 1% of the population—2.8 million people—to pray daily for the President. *The Presidential Prayer Team* is an independent, nonpartisan, nonprofit organization with the singular purpose of inciting daily prayer for the Office of the President, as well as providing information on the daily prayer needs of our country's leadership, for this and future administrations. Anyone may join. Membership is free.

Members receive a free official window decal, plus weekly presidential prayer updates
via email. To join the team visit: www.presidentialprayerteam.org

The Presidential Prayer Team • PO Box 2300 • Orange, CA 92859 • 1-800-295-1235

The Presidential Prayer Team is not associated with any political party, official, governmental office or religious denomination. It does not promote political, social, or commercial causes. It is a grassroots effort of individuals and churches around the nation who believe in the power of prayer to shape our nation's future.

Ordering Additional Copies

You may order additional copies of this book directly from The Pauline Hord Trust by mail if paying by check. If you would like to pay by credit card, you may order this book online from these secure websites: www.prayingforthepresident.com or www.masterdesign.org.

Total Items	Cost	Quantity	Total
1-9 copies	$15 each	_____	_____
10-49 copies	$12 each	_____	_____
50+ copies	$10 each	_____	_____
Tennessee residents add 9.25% sales tax			_____
Add shipping and handling cost (see below)			_____
(Payment must accompany order) **Total**			_____

Shipping & Handling
For 1st copy: $ 3.00
For each additional copy: add $.50 each
(if over 50 copies, add $.20 for each additional copy)

Name _____

Address _____

City, State, Zip _____

Phone _____

Email (optional) _____

Payment by check (# _____)

Payment by credit card is taken online.

The Pauline Hord Trust
2095 Exeter Rd #80-200
Germantown, TN 38138
www.prayingforthepresident.com
info@prayingforthepresident.com